PRAISE FOR
THE WELLBEING BOOK

"Andrew is an expert at improving workplaces and we should all heed his advice! Not only will you feel better, your workforce will be happier, and your business more profitable."

David C Watt, Executive Director, Institute of Directors

"This is not a book with lots of dos and don'ts, of musts and shoulds, adding to your long to-do list. It gently nudges you in the direction of paying more attention to your wellbeing by asking all the right questions. Sharman does not ask you to climb difficult mountains, but is your guide in an interesting garden, that is you. I am more directive than this: buy this book, read a chapter every day and take three minutes to reflect, undisturbed. If you invest more time and energy in your work than in your own wellbeing, you shouldn't be surprised that your work is doing better than you."

Professor Dr Theo Compernolle, Neuropsychiatrist and author of *BrainChains* and *Stress: Friend and Foe*

"A brilliant little book – easy to read, useful, practical and brimming with ideas. This is self-help with an edge – a must-read for anyone with a mind, body or soul."

Dom Jackman, Founder, Escape the City

"Having practised and assisted many on their leadership journey, it has become increasingly obvious that there is a direct correlation between how we all feel about ourselves and how we perform. The practice of wellness and wellbeing sound far too sensible to argue with, but not enough of us really practise and live it. Andrew Sharman has with his new book, *The Wellbeing Book*, made the art and science of wellbeing practical, fun and so easy to adopt. You will read it once just to get the whole gist of it, but read it again and again as the straightforward approach changes your lives and the lives of those you love for the better. A must-read for all those who love life."

René Carayol MBE, Broadcaster, Broadsheet Columnist and author of *Corporate Voodoo* and *Spike*

"This is an extraordinary book – a complete game-changer for motivation and influence. Provides practical and – more importantly – actionable advice on how to reach our most important goals while consistently achieving personal happiness and lifelong satisfaction."

Philippe Delquié, Professor of Decision Sciences, George Washington University, USA

"*The Wellbeing Book* is your road map to transforming your life in ways that you've never dared to dream. If you want to move from just being to truly living: start here. Sharman's words leap from the page, kick you in the ass, pierce your heart, and awaken your mind to take you on a magnificent journey of your own design. Get ready to be transformed!"

Dr Lucy Rattrie, Chartered Psychologist specializing in Health, Wellbeing & Resilience

"A fast, high-impact read with compelling anecdotes and great context in which to understand and improve your own wellbeing."

Dr Jens Meyer, Dean of the European Centre for Executive Development (CEDEP) & INSEAD adjunct faculty, Fontainebleau, France

"Simple, practical advice for time poor professionals looking to up their game when it comes to wellbeing. I challenge you to not find something in here that can change your life for the better – immediately. Written in a short, snappy and supportive style with plenty of actionable takeaways. As a wellbeing professional myself, I still found myself coming away with tons of ideas to implement in my own life. Do yourself a favour and pick up a copy right now!"

Hari Kalymnios, author of *The Thought Gym*

"Filled with wisdom, inspiration and practical ideas, all rooted in ground-breaking research. Sharman's positive strategies hold immense power and will change the way you view yourself, your life, your work, and the world. Essential reading."

Professor Sam Abadir, Professor of Negotiation and Conflict Management, IMD Business School, Lausanne, Switzerland

"A highly-informative, pragmatic and amiable style runs through this well-thought-out book which succinctly distils the plethora of information on this important topic to focus on what is most essential, not only to busy professionals, but anyone with an interest in improving their time on this planet. A must-read for everyone!"

Dave Stevenson, Global Director of Health & Safety, Pearson Plc.

"Wellbeing is not simply personal, but systemic too. By developing our subjective wellbeing we can make a tremendous positive impact on our communities, organisations and ultimately on wider society. Andrew Sharman's insightful and practical book will help you do just that."

Steven D'Souza, Associate Fellow, University of Oxford and co-author of *Not Knowing* and *Not Doing*

THE WELLBEING BOOK

50 WAYS TO MASTER YOUR MIND, BOOST YOUR BODY AND SUPERCHARGE YOUR SOUL

ANDREW SHARMAN

Published by
LID Publishing Limited
The Record Hall, Studio 204,
16-16a Baldwins Gardens,
London EC1N 7RJ, UK

524 Broadway, 11th Floor, Suite 08-120,
New York, NY 10012, US

info@lidpublishing.com
www.lidpublishing.com

A member of:

BPR
Business Publishers Roundtable

www.businesspublishersroundtable.com

© Andrew Sharman, 2019
© LID Publishing Limited, 2019

Printed in the Czech Republic by Finidr

ISBN: 978-1-911498-87-2

Cover and page design: Caroline Li & Matthew Renaudin

THE WELLBEING BOOK

50 WAYS TO MASTER YOUR MIND, BOOST YOUR BODY AND SUPERCHARGE YOUR SOUL

ANDREW SHARMAN

LONDON   NEW YORK   BOGOTA
MADRID   BARCELONA   BUENOS AIRES
MEXICO CITY   MONTERREY   SHANGHAI

FOR OTHER TITLES
IN THE SERIES...

CONCISE
ADVICE
LAB

SMALL
BOOKS:
BIG
IDEAS

CLEVER CONTENT, DYNAMIC IDEAS, PRACTICAL
SOLUTIONS AND ENGAGING VISUALS –
A CATALYST TO INSPIRE NEW WAYS OF THINKING
AND PROBLEM-SOLVING IN A COMPLEX WORLD

conciseadvicelab.com

To life's enthusiasts, the *bons vivants*.

And to Dad, the man of books,
with eternal thanks for my own wellbeing,
and for *everything else*.

CONTENTS

INTRODUCTION

HOW ARE YOU FEELING?

As the CEO of a boutique consulting, training and coaching business, I've been fortunate to work in more than 100 countries around the globe, with thousands of managers and leaders in many of the world's most admired corporations. As a professor of leadership and organizational culture at an elite business school in Europe, I share a classroom with some of the brightest minds and sharpest suits.

To each I ask the same question: "How are you feeling?"

Rarely do I get a response that stretches beyond a cursory "OK". Usually my words are met with a simple, silent smile. My question is received as a statement.

Around the world, cultural variations receive the same treatment. The British stiff upper lip lets out a terse "Fine" in reply. In South Africa, "Howzit?" now functions as a synonym for "Hello". In the US a warm "How-ya-doin'?" is met with a brief "Hey" or "Howdy". In Asia, on the other hand, the enquiry may be perceived as too personal to answer.

With thousands of these micro-experiments[1] under my belt, I can now only conclude that people either *don't like* being asked how they feel or, perhaps more unnervingly, that actually they don't *know* how they feel.

HEALTHY CITIZENS ARE THE GREATEST ASSET ANY COUNTRY CAN HAVE

On 21 March 1943, Prime Minister Winston Churchill uttered the above words as he elaborated his four-year plan for Britain, taking the opportunity to underline the importance of health, strength and vitality to a nation caught in a period of significant change. Churchill's words are as relevant today as they were back then.

As our lives get busier and busier, the boundaries between work and leisure blur and we spend less time thinking about what we're putting our ourselves through.

This fast living is resulting in a pandemic of 'ill-being': from general weariness and 'feeling under the weather' to prolonged bouts of sickness and lethargy and sharp increases in stress, depression and mental health issues.

Around one in four of people now experience a mental health issue in any given year. Depression is predicted to be a leading cause of disease burden by 2030.[2] And it starts young: 50% of people suffer their first bout of depression in adolescence or early adulthood, and 75% of people before they reach the of age 25.[3]

Cardiovascular diseases, cancer, diabetes and chronic lung diseases are now the four main causes of non-communicable disease death, making up around 70% of all deaths (around 17 million) across the world each year.[4] By the year 2030 the figure will top 24 million. Furthermore, the number of deaths from diabetes skyrocketed by 66% between 2000 and 2015.[5]

What's behind these statistics? It's us. How we live, what we do, who we are.

Although we know that smoking, alcohol, diet and exercise greatly impact our state of general health and wellbeing, we don't seem to be able to make the changes we need for good. Coronary heart disease and other types of cardiovascular disease now cause a third of all deaths globally each year (that's around 15 million people), and the number is rising. Simple changes to the way we live would reverse this trend.

The world in which we live and work is growing. The population has more than doubled since Churchill's call to arms. There's more than 7 billion of us now, and experts predict a rise to 10 billion by the year 2050. We're generally living longer too – and working longer. Retirement ages in many countries are already being extended, and the majority of us (unless we win the lottery) can expect to be working well into our seventies and perhaps even eighties.

The real purpose of this little book, then, is to bring the mind, body and soul back into balance and alignment; to help you explore simple ways to navigate and map your life, enhance your energy, boost your wellbeing, manage stress and enjoy a happier, longer and more fulfilling time on this planet.

I'll cut through the scientific research and guide you through 50 ideas to master your mind, boost your body and supercharge your soul. By the time you reach the end of the book, I hope that you'll see that it isn't that difficult to live a life of wellbeing, and I hope you'll feel that some of the ideas shared in this book are worth trying – because, after all, you're a human *being*, not just a human *doing*!

Are you ready?

Come on then, let's crack on!

Andrew Sharman
Switzerland, September 2018

HOW TO USE THIS BOOK

Yes, I know you know *how* to read, because you've got this book in your hand already. But here's the thing: there are several ways you might actually *go about* reading this book.

First, you could bash along like it's a normal book, starting at the first page and then keeping on turning the pages until you get to the end.

You might have a particular interest and prefer to focus only on one of the sections. That's cool too.

You could read one idea each day for 50 days and *essayer* (to try out) the connected activity each day as you read.

Or you could mix it up a little and just dip in and out at random. The *essays* are not in a specific formal order, so feel free to have some fun and bounce around with them.

There aren't really any rules – it's your book, after all! However you choose to read this book, have fun with it. Life's too short!

It's commonly believed that the American writer Mark Twain said: "The secret of getting ahead is getting started. The secret of getting started is breaking down your complex, overwhelming tasks into smaller manageable tasks, and then starting on the first one."

So, where will *you* start?

PART ONE

WELLBEING

A WORD ON WELLBEING

In 1948 the World Health Organization set out its constitution and defined 'health' as "a state of complete physical, mental and social well-being and not merely the absence of disease or infirmity".[6]

This definition set solid foundations for future dialogue and action on health – at work and within society at large. Beyond this it also introduced the concept of 'wellbeing' to the world.

Beyond those big killers mentioned in the Introduction to this book, the World Health Organization reckons that the greatest future risk to our wellbeing, satisfaction with life and personal productivity is dysthymia. Go on, have a guess what that is.

Dysthymia is defined as a sharp and distinct loss of energy that damages valuable social relationships, causes self-doubt and knocks dents in our feelings of happiness and contentment while nudging us further into mild yet chronic depression.[7]

Dysthymia comes directly from the way we live and is thought to affect more than 200 million of us. The good news, though, is that dysthymia is treatable. The really great news? It's *curable*! The bonus? This book will share 50 ways to help you beat it.

In the knowledge era, we often know what we should do to improve our wellbeing. But, even with the right skills, knowledge and behaviours, if we don't have energy, then our batteries are flat and our light and power are weak.

So how do we recharge the batteries? What's the power source? It's our wellbeing – our physical health, emotional health and mental health; our sense of purpose; and the meaning of our lives.

1. WHAT EXACTLY IS WELLBEING?

A common term nowadays, wellbeing is essentially a composite measure of how good we feel and how much we feel able to cope with what everyday life throws at us.

While it's hard to find consensus on a single definition, there is agreement in the research that, at a minimum, wellbeing includes the presence of positive emotions and moods (such as happiness, contentment and pride), the absence of negative emotions (such as anxiety and depression) and having a sense of satisfaction with life.[8]

In simple terms, it's how *happy*, *contented*, *comfortable* and *satisfied* we are. How *effectively we function*. Naturally it's personal and subjective – *it's all about us*.

Our wellbeing is dynamic in that it changes from moment to moment, day to day, month to month and even year to year.

Our wellbeing has a direct impact on our lives, with studies showing that wellbeing is linked to our life span, healthy behaviours, mental and physical illness, and productivity. Higher levels of wellbeing are associated with decreased risk of disease, illness and injury. Folks with good wellbeing have stronger immune systems, recover from illness and injury quicker, are more productive at work, contribute more to their communities, and tend to live longer and more happily too.

So, what influences our wellbeing?

Well, of course, our genes play a part: there's evidence to suggest that we may inherit part of our general wellbeing from our parents. But where we live; what we do for work; the money we earn, spend and save; the relationships we have with our friends, family and others; and our diet and exercise all play important (some say more important) roles.

Because wellbeing is personal and subjective, it is typically measured through self-report tools such as surveys and questionnaires. So, have a go at the exercise on the next page and let's see where your wellbeing is at right now.

Answer each question[9] honestly. Work briskly and go with your gut feeling, rating your response on a scale of one (low) to five (high).

1. How *well* do you feel right now?

2. How *happy* have you felt over the past 30 days?

3. Do you feel you have *meaning* in your life?

4. Do you feel you have sufficient *emotional and social support* in your life?

5. How *satisfied* are you with your life nowadays?

Remember that wellbeing is subjective and ever-changing. This little exercise gives you a quick snapshot of where you are *right now*. It's not a scientific study, so don't dwell too much on the actual scores; instead use the exercise to think about where you might like to get a boost in your wellbeing. Then read on!

You can return to these questions again later, and you might also want to keep your scores in mind as your progress through this book, allowing your responses to guide your focus as you read.

2. START WITH WHY

In his best-selling book *Start With Why*[10] and in a mega-million -times-watched TED Talk,[11] Simon Sinek explains why some people are significantly more inventive, pioneering and successful than others. I don't want to give the game away here, but he reckons it's because these people start with 'why'.

While Sinek's book is directed at organizational leaders, his thesis stands true for individual use when we think about wellbeing too. We'll get to that, but first let's understand his perspective.

Sinek reckons that most folks know *what* to do – a company is able to describe the products it makes, and workers are able to describe the job function they have. Some organizations and people know *how* to do what they do, in that they have a certain unique selling point or value proposition that sets them apart in what they make or do.

But the missing detail for Sinek is the *why*. He argues that most organizations and leaders today cannot clearly articulate *why* they do *what* they do.

Now, let's flip this from business to the topic of this book. You probably know *what* to do to improve your wellbeing (eat better, drink less alcohol, drink more water, spend more time with family and friends, get a life coach, see a shrink, go to church, take a trip, throw a party, etc.) and you very likely have a pretty good idea of *how* you should do these things too. But are you really clear on your *why*?

Sinek introduces what he calls the Golden Circle, a concept inspired by the golden ratio – a mathematical relationship that has had architects, artists, scientists, naturists and many more in rapture since the start of time. Leonardo da Vinci believed that the golden ratio provided a formula for proportion and beauty. Pharaohs used it to build pyramids. Pepsi adhere to it in their classic logo design.

The concept of the Golden Circle is much simpler than complex calculations – Sinek advocates that we must start from the inside and work out. We must start with why.

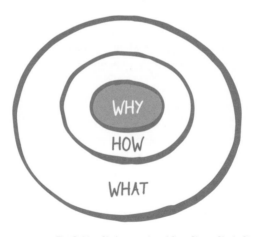

The Golden Circle, reproduced from Simon Sinek, *Start with Why: How Great Leaders Inspire Everyone to Take Action* (London: Penguin, 2009).

Over the course of this book, we'll explore ideas on both the what and the how. For now, to get started on the right track, we'll do what Sinek says and focus on the why. Answer the following questions as honestly and as concisely as you can.

Why did you pick up this book?

_____

_____

_____

_____

Why is your wellbeing important to you?

_____

_____

_____

_____

Why will you commit to reading this book?

_____

_____

_____

_____

3. WORKING WELL?

Most of us spend a large chunk of our lives working, so it makes sense to consider how our wellbeing is influenced by our work.

Whether we're a blue-chip boss, a senior manager or an hourly paid employee, we can be certain that our work affects our wellbeing and our wellbeing affects our work.

In the UK, a report published by the Department for Work and Pensions (DWP) shows that "the UK faces a significant mental health challenge at work".[12] The report reveals that 15% of people at work today have symptoms of mental health conditions. Around 300,000 people with long-term mental health problems lose their jobs every year – and at a much higher rate than those with physical health conditions.

The DWP report shows the significant cost of poor mental health to UK businesses and the economy as a whole. Poor mental health costs employers between £33 billion and £42 billion a year, with an annual cost to the UK economy of between £74 billion and £99 billion.

In the UK, 131 million working days are lost every year to sickness absence – that's almost five days for every worker. Musculoskeletal conditions (such as back and joint pain), coughs and colds, and stress, anxiety and depression account for more than half of these days.

One in every four British workers have a physical health condition that has lasted more than a year. One in eight report a mental health issue.

Nearly 50% of employees with a current health condition feel that it affects their ability to do their job. And a report by the Institute of Leadership & Management concludes that only two in every five employees are working at peak performance.[13]

It's abundantly clear: the way we're working isn't working.

During his tenure, UK Prime Minister David Cameron made a speech suggesting there was more to life than work and that it was time to focus "not just on GDP, but also GWB – General Well-Being".[14] Pretty quickly afterwards, the United Nations General Assembly called on member states to give more focus to happiness and wellbeing when measuring social and economic development.

While the research tends to shy away from quantifying exact returns on investment, there are many corporate case studies that reveal there is a solid pay-off for companies that think about the wellbeing of their people.

More and more organizations today are beginning to understand that good wellbeing at work can:

- **Increase motivation and productivity** – happy and healthy workers have more energy and can perform better physically and mentally. They're also more alert, focused and efficient.
- **Build morale and boost teamwork** – wellbeing activities provide opportunities for people to engage with others around a shared purpose or interest, which helps to build friendship and team spirit.
- **Decrease feelings of pressure and work-related stress** – as information overload continues and the world of work gets smaller and faster, enhanced wellbeing will help us to manage stress and boost resilience.

Wellbeing at work is more than just bowls of fruit and reduced-price gym memberships (though these may be helpful). To get the balance right, organizations need to consider how they both affect and promote workers' emotional, mental and physical health and wellbeing. But, of course, individuals need to take responsibility too – and that's presumably why you've picked up this book in the first place.

The ideas are limitless and can range from mindfulness training to chill-out rooms, from open offices to collaboration spaces. Community volunteering, health lunch clubs and walking meetings can all boost cohesion and interaction amongst teams. Onsite gyms or yoga classes, a dedicated walking or running track, and bike-to-work schemes all help to encourage physical wellbeing. Similarly, remote working, flexible work hours and 'duvet days' may all help to increase mental capacity, creative thinking and a sense of being in control.

Of course, wellbeing activities at work depend on what feels right, what fits the culture and what might appeal to employees. So let's think about this in a bit more detail:

- How seriously does your employer take your wellbeing? Do you feel there's a range of activities available to help you be your best at work every day? If not, what would you like to see? Now's the time to make suggestions to your boss!
- If you manage or lead a team at work, what do you think about the wellbeing of your people? If your team members answered the questions in the previous chapter, what would the results tell you?
- What opportunities do you have at work to increase motivation and teamwork and decrease the potential for work-related stress?

4. STOP!

So far in this book, we've set the stage for thinking about the importance of our health, introduced the concept of wellbeing, and explored what influences how happy, healthy, comfortable and satisfied we feel in life.

You've also worked out *why* this is important to you. A great start!

But now, before you get any further into reading this book, before we get to the *what* and *how*, before you even turn another page, I'd like you to *stop*.

Take a moment right now – just for yourself – to check in a little more deeply on your own wellbeing in this very moment.

Try to clearly define your response to each question: be as accurate as you can.

Even just one word will do.

Before you write anything, though – before pen even touches paper – take a solid 60 seconds to consider each question fully. Start the clock.

How do you feel today?

_____

What's on your mind?

_____

How do you treat your body?

_____

How nourished is your soul?

_____

How would you *like* to feel?

_____

While these questions may appear superficial, they actually dig deeper than the simple check in we did together in Chapter 1. You'll notice that here we start with a thought on your general well-being, and then move forward to consider your mind, your body and your soul.

As we continue our journey together in this book, we'll follow the same path. So, if there's an answer above that sets alarm bells ringing for you, you may want to flick forward to the equivalent section of the book now.

"A ruffled mind makes a restless pillow."

– Charlotte Brontë

MIND

A WORD ON THE MIND

As a kid, I wasn't big on television.

I forsook cartoons, *Blue Peter* and the Australian soap opera *Neighbours* for a show I never believed I'd be interested in. Even today, looking back, I'm amazed I passed up Colt Seavers in *The Fall Guy* (a very big deal for me, aspiring as I was to be a stuntman, like Colt) for a show where an ageing gent swivelled around in his chair to ask members of the public a series of random questions.

Mastermind has been running on British TV since 1972, and as that menacing theme tune kicked in I could hardly wait for Magnus Magnusson to look down his nose and ask the first question.

As humans, we're addicted to questions. Our minds love to work. Look around you on the bus, train or plane – how many passengers are locked into crosswords, sudoku, word searches, *Tetris*, *Candy Crush*, etc.?

David Adam, talking in his memoir on his own obsessive compulsive disorder, is remarkably erudite:

> The mind is a thought factory. Every day it processes a conveyor belt of thousands of thoughts, good and bad, happy and sad, useful and intrusive. The factory must decide how to act on them and then issue instructions to respond. We each do this differently, based on our unique combinations of early experience, environment, and biology; our biases, preconceptions, and knowledge. The conveyor belt always rolls and new thoughts arrive in a constant stream. Something always comes in and something always goes out.[15]

The actor Anthony Hopkins reckons that, "We are dying from overthinking. We are slowly killing ourselves by thinking about everything. Think. Think. Think. You can never trust the human mind anyway. It's a death trap."[16] He may not be far wrong.

In the UK, the cost of work-related stress to society is now around £4 billion per year. In the US, over 1 million workers call in sick complaining of stress *every day*, generating a cost to employers of over $200 billion. Even this number pales when compared to the total amount spent on healthcare – a whopping $2.7 trillion in the US each year.

Mental health issues such as stress and depression are on the rise in every developed nation around the world. One in every six adults now experience a common mental health problem every week, with the most common diagnosis being a mixture of anxiety and depression.

MIND FULL, OR MINDFUL?

A recent study of 15,000 people revealed that most people spend 46.9% of their waking hours thinking about something other than what they're doing, and this mind-wandering typically makes them unhappy.[17]

The study says: "A human mind is a wandering mind, and a wandering mind is an unhappy mind. The ability to think about what is not happening is a cognitive achievement that comes at an emotional cost."[18]

We've got to focus!

'Mindfulness' is about training the brain to block out the myriad distractions and worries that invade our thoughts, to allow us to live in the moment. Practitioners of mindfulness find it has a positive impact on their mental health, aiding them in effectively managing stress and negative thoughts.

Mindfulness is now becoming more popular in the corporate world. These days, many occupations require multitasking – and often this means that our thoughts become scattered and jump from place to place. This not only tends to negatively affect productivity but also exhausts the mind.

Nobel Laureate Herbert A. Simon warned us about this back in 1969:

> In an information-rich world, the wealth of information means a dearth of something else: a scarcity of whatever it is that information consumes. What information consumes is rather obvious

– it consumes the attention of its recipients. Hence a wealth of information creates a poverty of attention, and a need to allocate that attention efficiently among the overabundance of information sources that might consume it.[19]

Simon was writing in a different age, of course, but his words are perfectly relevant today with the flood of information on social media, news feeds and so on.

When we're overwhelmed, we become stressed – and, in these situations, we need to take a moment for ourselves and focus on something positive.

During a busy day, taking time out might sound counterintuitive – but, if we don't, our brains won't refresh. As a consequence, we'll fail to manage stress, and opportunities to reflect and gain new insight will be lost. Research published by the Mental Health Foundation in the UK has determined that practising mindfulness can enhance mental wellbeing,[20] aid concentration, improve our ability to learn new things and increase our personal efficiency.[21]

So, let's see how we can master our minds.

5. BUT FIRST, COFFEE

I had a great coffee this morning. No, I mean *really* great. In fact, it was *amazing*.

It was at this little place I know in Venice Beach, Los Angeles. As it became my turn to order, it was clear that the barista already knew what my order would be so, rather than asking, he started to tell me about the beans.

As he described the different kinds of coffee beans, I was transported back to a moment in Addis Ababa, last year, sitting cross-legged in front of burning embers as a beautiful woman in a gold-coloured *habesha kemis* – the traditional dress – entranced me with her coffee ceremony.

Mindfulness is like that – it is the miracle that can call back in a flash our dispersed mind and restore it to wholeness so that we can live each moment of life.

Cup in hand I sit on a bench in the street and the 7am Californian sunshine washes over me. I'm alive.

When we find ourselves in a familiar place – stumbling to the shower, driving to work on autopilot, hunched over our laptops, drifting through meetings – it can be difficult to be present, can't it? It's because our brains are in a routine we've become accustomed to in which our central processor makes things easy for us, taking us from A to B to C without us having to compute. But that's not *living*. It's *surviving*.

Only when we step out of our routine can we begin to notice the way it feels to really appreciate the taste of our coffee. We notice we're here. It's an experience our brains need to stop for and to process. Instead of just *doing*, how about just *being* in the moment for once?

We live our lives the way we choose to live them. Don't wait for a break in your routine in order to do something meaningful – start today. Start small. Take *this moment* as a brand-new moment in your life. You'll never get this moment back again, so, whatever you're doing, get curious! Get ready to be amazed.

How does your coffee taste? Is it simply fuel for a tired mind, or does it conjure up some kind of experience in your brain? Where are the moments for you to be truly mindful in your life today? Choose one, focus in and get ready to be amazed.

6. A CALL TO ATTENTION

In research reported in *TIME* magazine, researchers in Canada used electroencephalography to study the brain activity of 2,000 people and found that the average human attention span dropped from 12 seconds in the year 2000 to 8 seconds in 2015.[22] Compare this to the humble goldfish, with an attention span of 9 seconds – even though it's swum past that plastic bridge and fake plant thousands of times.

With the advent of social media, our minds have evolved to adapt to the information flood created by the synergy between news media and social media. Traditional newspapers are falling in popularity relative to the short, sharp bursts of information provided by internet news streams and social media channels.

In 2014, Mashable became one of the most-used online news feeds. In response, Associated Press – the world's biggest independent news organization – called for its reporters to limit their articles to 300–500 words.[23]

We've become addicted to fast facts. Recent studies have revealed that 77% of people aged 18–35 reported that "when nothing is occupying my attention, the first thing I do is reach for my phone".[24]

Despite our ability to remain present and focused having decreased, our ability to multitask has improved in this mobile age, as we hop from input to input gathering information. Yet, if we can't concentrate as much, doesn't this simply mean we try to do more things but less effectively?

Ted Selker, researcher at MIT, reckons so: "Our attention span gets affected by the way we do things. If we spend our time flitting from one thing to another on the web, we get into a habit of not concentrating."[25]

Experts estimate that between 20,000 and 50,000 thoughts are processed by our brains each day. How can we be sure that we pay attention to the important ones and make the right decisions?

Attention is the process by which our brains decide what is important, from the constant flow of information they receive. External distractions (such as stress, an attractive stranger on the way to work, a bright red Ferrari zooming past or the ping of our mobile message function) and internal distractions (such as our mind wandering) diminish the power of our attention. It's believed that distractions cause our minds to wander up to 50% of the time.[26]

Why? Because it's learnt to suck up information from everywhere, and because it needs a break from the barrage of information we give it.

So today, why not make a quick list of three things you'd like to learn something about? Perhaps a news item, a sport or hobby, a person or a potential place for your next vacation. Try to resist being distracted by your smartphone or Wikipedia, or opening a stack of pages on the internet. Instead, deliberately focus your attention on the task in hand – and beat that goldfish!

1. _____

_____

_____

_____

2. _____

_____

_____

_____

3. _____

_____

_____

_____

7. FEELING THE HEAT

In recent years you've probably noticed the increase in popularity of books on some simple ideas.

First, a dominant theme of getting back to nature – often through the medium of wood: see, for example, *Swedish Carving Techniques*, *The Wood Fire Handbook*, *A Guide to Spoon Carving* and many more.

Second is a focus on living a simpler life. The best-selling *Cabin Porn*[27] is a seductive little book that has grown adults (including myself) sneaking off to a quiet, comfy corner to drool over it, while *Van Life* promotes a life on the road exploring nature at your own pace in a debt-free lifestyle.

At this point it would be natural to ponder whether all these books encouraging self-reliance and getting back to nature point towards some sort of impending apocalypse. I'd rather believe that they've grown in popularity simply because many of us have a deep desire to get back to basics. To be more authentic. To find peace, and to escape the din of modern life.

This isn't new. It's merely a reflection of a deep human need. As polar explorer Erling Kagge points out, "there's something slow and sustainable about such pursuits, something meditative" that makes them attractive to us.[28] A quiet moment, often alone, to truly relish the task at hand.

Whether you're whittling a spoon, adding yeast to your home brew, knitting a pair of socks or swinging an axe to split logs for your fire, these activities use your hands to *create something*. And, through this act of creation, you become mindfully engaged in the pursuit of subtle achievement. The feelings of satisfaction generated are not things that can be bought from any store. They are enjoyment in its purest sense.

Today, find a simple activity, *something slow and sustainable, something meditative*, that you can really set your mind to. Try to focus not on any particular result but rather on the process itself. Notice the action, the energy, the rhythm. Listen to the sounds around you. Feel the heat. And then, finally, really *enjoy* the achievement.

8. TURN OFF, TUNE OUT

We are bombarded with information every day of our lives.

News, TV, radio, billboards, social media and online advertisements; – there are literally tens of thousands of inputs invading our lives on a daily basis. As well as being practically inescapable, these inputs are exerting an influence.

Think about a time when you engaged in a discussion with someone on a topic you consider important. No doubt you were aware you were entering it. You probably came equipped with a point of view, and, if you were influenced by the other person's ideas, it will have been because of the strength and persuasiveness of their argument.

In contrast, the influence of those different external sources is far more insidious – and works at a largely unconscious level.

Even when we are aware of the inputs, we are still largely powerless to do anything about them. They come unbidden into our lives from a variety of sources and there are often just too many of them, and too many variables.

However, there are usually two points during the day when we might be able to escape the buzz of background interference and tune out: first thing in the morning and last thing at night.

Bookend your day with carefully thought-out rituals to start it successfully and end it with a great night's sleep. It will make a world of difference.

Here are some rituals you might want to consider integrating into your routine:

- **Tune out.** Whether you're engaging with or disengaging from the world, enjoy a few minutes away from the noise. No texts, emails, social media, news, radio or internet. Spend some time thinking about a positive thing you can do that day, or reflecting on some of the things for which you are thankful.
- **Do something for yourself.** Whether it's meditation, prayer, journaling or taking some deep, structured, diaphragmatic breaths, be good to yourself for a few minutes.
- **Read something that inspires you.** This might be a few pages on a subject you enjoy or have specialist knowledge of. Reading a little every day will boost your expertise in your chosen field as you keep up to date with best practice and the latest thinking.
- **Move your body.** Even if it's only for five minutes. In the morning, do a few cardio exercises, such as star jumps or running on the spot. At the end of the day, try a couple of minutes of stretching or light yoga moves. Just moving your body will stimulate your lymphatic drainage system and move toxins out.

9. LOST IN A MOMENT

In the modern workplace, there seems to be an obsession with hiring workers who are proficient at 'multitasking'.

Presumably, this comes from business owners pushing for maximum efficiency from their staff. Nevertheless, in practice this can be myopic, naturally promoting rushed and badly executed tasks, poor focus and stressful working conditions.

The practice of doing 'just one activity' – or *ichigyo zammai* in Japanese – is the foundation of mindful practice, and being focused on a particular task can be a major eliminator of stress.

Whether you're a barista making coffee or a blacksmith working at a forge, when you're locked in that process, you're entirely encapsulated by it. Everything else – all the personal and emotional baggage that we carry around and that pervades our minds like background noise – dims for just a moment.

Mindfulness has the power to turn a humdrum task into something that brings us pleasure.

Take an everyday activity such as doing the washing up or reading a newspaper; if we immerse ourselves in these tasks fully, we can actually find refuge in them.

Zen Buddhist master Shunryu Suzuki believed that concentration on a single act is the first step in attaining mindfulness. He said: "Instead of having some object of worship, we just concentrate on the activity which we do in each moment. When you bow, just bow; when you sit, just sit; when you eat, just eat."[29]

Focusing on just one activity can be a difficult thing to master – but it isn't completely outside your control. Like any skill or ability, it's developed over time.

The following exercises might get you going:

- **Assess your daily routine.** Spend some time evaluating your attention as it grows and declines throughout the day. When does it spike? When does it drop off? What outside influences cause it to deteriorate? Does tiredness stop you getting started? Do you struggle to regain your momentum after lunch? Are you endlessly distracted by social media? Does boredom get the better of you? Is your workplace too distracting? Find out what factors positively influence your focus and try to extend your peak periods.
- **Take time out.** Take a few minutes each day to do something for yourself – to free your mind from distractions. Doing this regularly will increase your ability to keep a clear head and deal more successfully with stressful situations.
- **Exercise.** Scientific studies demonstrate a correlation between physical exercise and the ability to concentrate. A quick work-out – or even a quick stroll – during your lunch break will boost your focus and give your mind the chance to release the mental and physical stresses typically built up throughout your working day.

10. ALL THE SMALL THINGS

Let's rewind to the 1990s.

Imagine the scene – you're in downtown New York City, parking your car, on the way to meet a friend for a meal. Before locking up, you pull your stereo from the dashboard, leaving the wires exposed and hanging from the gaping void. A sticker on your windscreen reads 'No Stereo' in an effort to deter thieves. As you cross the road, litter breezes past your feet like tumbleweed.

Meanwhile, down the street, people jump the turnstile of the underground station to ride for free, while youths tag buildings – from busy stores to residential homes – with their latest graffiti.

Back then, violent crime in NYC was at peak levels. Newly installed mayor Rudy Giuliani had big problems.

But when social scientist George Kelling strolled into the mayor's office he brought answers.

Small answers.

Kelling explained that leaving minor issues unfixed – such as broken windows, litter and graffiti – leads to more serious problems as local residents change the way they see their community.

This deterioration of community modifies the way folks behave when it comes to their communal space which, in turn, breaks down community control. As rowdiness, drunkenness and drug-taking seep into a community, they signify that the community can't assert informal social control, and citizens become afraid that worse things will happen. In an attempt to stay safe, a once-cohesive community falls apart as individuals and families retreat to the safety of their own homes and spend less time in communal areas to avoid the risk of attacks by strangers. With problems left unchecked, locals become less inclined to go out and become less connected to their community.

Kelling's 'broken windows' theory is a criminological construct of behavioural norm-setting that suggests maintaining and monitoring urban environments to prevent small crimes helps to create an atmosphere of law and order that prevents more serious crimes occurring.

Giuliani took some convincing but gave Kelling a chance. Within weeks of the introduction of policies requiring rapid response to fixing smashed windows, cleaning graffiti and holding fare dodgers to account, things began to change. Local pride began to grow again, residents gradually spent more time in public places and community inclusion returned. In Mayor Giuliani's term, violent crime in New York dropped 56%, murder fell 65%, robbery declined 67% and aggravated assault came down by almost a third.[30]

The turnaround in New York teaches us that we don't have to focus on the big things. Small steps in the right direction all add up.

The broken windows theory has been applied well beyond the realms of urban decay – for example, to improve student behaviour in schools, to boost economic regeneration and to cure substance addiction.

In the corporate world, Paul O'Neill turned American aluminium giant Alcoa around with what he referred to as "small questions."[31] And every employee of the world's fastest Formula One racing team (from designers and engineers to office clerks and team leaders) shares a common objective to reduce each race time by 0.1 of a second.

And so, over to you. Diet, exercise, nutrition, personal education, a new career or a new relationship – where might your broken windows be? What small things can you focus on right now to improve your life?

11. DEGREES OF SEPARATION

Doris Day is famously once supposed to have once said that "wrinkles are hereditary – parents get them from their children".

Well, it seems, if you're male at least, this might well be reciprocal.

Researchers at the University of Oxford examined data from more than 52,000 people, surveyed within family groups in 28 European countries, with parents and children divided according to educational accomplishments.[32]

The results showed that men whose academic achievements were at a lower level than their parents were discovered to be twice as likely to be psychologically distressed than those who had attained a similar level of education. Furthermore, men who had significantly fallen short of their parents' academic accomplishments were shown to be a staggering 50% more likely to suffer psychological distress.

Interestingly, the research revealed that the psychological condition of the women who were surveyed seemed to be little affected by failing to match the level of their parents' educational achievements.

It is not the case that women care less about their education or are less competitive; rather, men seem to be considerably more likely to attribute 'success' to personal endeavours and base this on their own merits. As a result, men tend to spend much of their lives wrestling with an unconscious desire to do better than their parents. If they don't manage it, they struggle to cope with the perceived material failing. Women, on the other hand, seem to have few such hang-ups about their parents' achievements.

Whatever your gender, the human psyche is a strange thing. There are myriad factors that shape our motivations and self-belief from a number of sources – some nature, some nurture and many of them working at an entirely subconscious level.

If you want to accentuate your self-belief and minimize your psychological stress, try the following:

- **Write down your accomplishments** and refer to them regularly – remembering to update your list when you succeed at something new. Look for patterns in your successes to help you identify and understand your skills.
- **Talk to the people who love you.** Very often, people struggle to see their strengths or identify their best traits. As a result, talking with friends can often be both illuminating and surprising.
- **Find a cause.** It can be difficult to believe in yourself if you spend your life doing things to fit in with people. Doing more things that you believe in will bring out your passion and help you work harder and achieve more – which will inevitably lead to less stress and a greater sense of achievement.

12. DIGITAL DETOX

Digital distractions are sweeping through our lives like wildfire.

In 2016, Nielsen reported that we spend 127 minutes per day on our smartphones, 63 minutes on tablets, 126 minutes on the laptop and 117 minutes watching TV.[33]

Our smartphones are now the biggest source of disruption to daily life – even when we're not looking at them. Push notifications, texts and emails just keep on coming.

Myriad reports tell us that one in three adults now regularly check their phones during the night, 79% of smartphone owners check their device within 15 minutes of waking and 30% check it while on the loo.[34] Forensic cyberpsychologist Dr Mary Aitken reckons we now check our phones 200 times a day[35] – that's every seven minutes!

But we love it! According to a Facebook survey, one-third of all Americans would rather give up sex than their phones.[36]

However, this tech addiction is creating havoc with our minds, bodies and souls – zapping our attention, smashing our productivity and playing havoc with our sleep as a result of all the blue light our screens produce.

If you fancy a digital detox, here are some ideas to get you started:

- Self-impose a ban on device use for the first hour on waking and the last hour of the day.
- Stash your smartphone in your bag or case at the start of meetings.
- Set your device to 'flight mode' when you need to focus on a task or project.
- Create an email filter that moves mail with certain keywords to a separate folder: make the keywords 'unsubscribe', 'manage your account' and 'privacy policy' and you'll see a vast reduction in your junk mails.[37]
- Set regular times when you check your mail – maybe two or three times a day at dedicated times.

And, if you're feeling radical, try the following:

- Unfollow everyone on Twitter for one week. Refollow only those you actively miss.
- Change your smartphone for a simple handheld device that only handles texts and calls.

13. FORWARD THINKING

The modern business world moves quickly.

Many people feel themselves falling behind if they're not constantly learning and acquiring new skills. New technologies continually reshape the work environment and greater levels of automation mean competition amongst workers is greater than ever.

In a growing number of industries and professions, workers today – just like sharks – need to keep moving forward to survive.

Knowledge has become a form of currency. However, unlike money, when you use knowledge, you retain it. It's possible to transfer knowledge anywhere in the world instantly and for free. And it comes with a degree of reverence and respect that money on its own rarely attains. Consequently, it forms the basis of more authentic relationships.

At a personal level, knowledge helps you accomplish your goals faster and gives you a sense of satisfaction when you do. It aids working memory, helping connections within the brain speed up, making you a better communicator and improving your levels of self-confidence.

Learning also helps to develop abstract thinking, allowing you to think outside the box and beyond personal circumstances.

Many successful and inspirational public figures – including Microsoft founder Bill Gates, Apple visionary Steve Jobs, and scientist and author Stephen Hawking – have all advocated lifelong learning as the secret to success.

Former US President Barack Obama once disclosed in an interview with the *New York Times* that during his time in office he made sure that he read for an hour each day. He claimed it gave him the ability to "slow down and get perspective" and "get in somebody else's shoes".[38]

The part of the brain that deals with learning responds to new stimuli by rewarding you with dopamine – the happy hormone. We also receive a further rush of dopamine when we finish our learning activity.

So, try to devote some time each day to acquiring new knowledge. You can do this in any number of ways – reading a book or a broadsheet newspaper, or learning about the latest developments in a chosen area of interest. If you're feeling tired after a long day, you can learn in a more passive way. Listen to the radio or a podcast, or watch a documentary on TV.

There are a lot of good things on the Discovery Channel, too – incidentally, you can learn a lot from watching sharks.

14. THANKSGIVING

We all struggle, from time to time, to see the good things in life.

When we're continually bombarded by shocking news headlines, targeted by advertising campaigns imposing perceived ideals upon us, or simply lost in the frenetic pace of the modern world, it can be difficult to step back and see life for how it really is.

Mindfulness is about paying closer attention to our thoughts – and, as we do so, learning to appreciate the good things in life.

Next time you're stuck in a traffic jam, instead of fretting about your lateness and your distance from your intended journey, focus on where you are instead. As you do, you'll start to notice the melody of the song playing on the car radio and the beauty of the patchwork fields that lie beyond the motorway as you gaze out of the window ...

Researchers from the University of California conducted a study of 1,000 people in which they tested the effects of gratitude.[39] Participants were split into two groups: one group was asked to keep a journal in which they wrote down five positive things that happened to them each day; the other group had to write down five negative things.

Positive examples included the generosity of loved ones and the sense of euphoria felt when engaging with nature. Examples of negative things included difficulty in finding a parking space and – yep – getting stuck in traffic.

Those who kept the positive journals experienced significant psychological, physical and social benefits, as well as reporting a rise in overall health and wellbeing. In contrast, the group who concentrated on the negative aspects of their daily lives saw all these things decline.

When we become more mindful, we open ourselves up to all aspects of experience – both positive and negative. We see ourselves, others and the world around us with a greater sense of curiosity and wonder. Being grateful transforms our outlook on life, bringing renewed vigour and a better understanding of our sense of place.

Take a moment to consider some of the good things in your life right now. List five positive things in the space over the page:

1. _____

_____

_____

2. _____

_____

_____

3. _____

_____

_____

4. _____

_____

_____

5. _____

_____

_____

Now reflect on your list. How do you feel?

_____

_____

_____

15. ANCHORS AWAY!

Neuro-linguistic programming (NLP) is a theory based around a set of tools and techniques that can help us to deal with unhelpful patterns in our thinking, beliefs and behaviour. It can also help to introduce new positive and constructive ways to master our minds and turbocharge our lives.

A central thread of NLP is that our minds are great at creating memories of important life moments.

These moments – referred to as 'anchors' in NLP speak – can trigger happy memories, which can, in turn, stimulate positive behaviours.

Anchors might be particular smells – such as the perfume of a loved one that takes you back to your first date, or a special home-cooked recipe that reminds you of when you were growing up. They might also be sounds or even visual imagery.

NLP can help in just three steps:

1. Choose the emotional state you want to be in – energetic, calm, happy, etc. – and concentrate on this.
2. Now recall a time when you were in this state – perhaps running a race, chilling on the sofa or on a special vacation.
3. Think of a particular movement, phrase, sound or image you can associate with this emotional state – maybe a thumbs-up, a picture of a beach or a big smile. This is your anchor.
4. Now practise setting this anchor. Each time you want to return to the emotional state you were in, just concentrate on doing the movement, uttering the words or making the sound. (Maybe *that's* why those tennis pros make that noise).[40]

16. HITTING THE HIGH NOTES

Psychologist Dan Gilbert suggests that all humans have a psychological immune system that helps us to feel better and synthesizes happiness.[41]

Listening to our favourite music is a popular way to relax and unwind, but researchers at Serbia's University of Niš have found that listening to music actually releases hormones that actively cause the synthesized happiness Gilbert mentions.[42] The researchers also found that listening to music was effective at improving vascular health, with our veins literally enjoying a workout as endorphins (one of a number of brain chemicals that transmit electrical signals in our nervous systems) are produced and flow through our system.

To test their hypotheses, the researchers split 74 patients with cardiovascular disease into three groups. Group A was given an exercise routine to follow for three weeks. Group B followed the same exercise routine but in addition were instructed to listen to their favourite music for 30 minutes every day. Group C listened only to music and did not participate in exercise.

At the end of the programme, the participants in Group A were found to have boosted vital measures of heart functionality significantly and increased their capacity for exercise by 29%. The participants in Group B, following the regime of exercise and music, were observed to have increased their exercise capacity by 39%. Curiously, even Group C, who did not undertake any exercise during the trial but simply listened to half an hour of their favourite music each day, improved their capacity by 19%!

While these conclusions offer an interesting perspective on the enhancement of wellbeing, the findings are not exactly new. Around 2,800 years ago, simple musical patterns were found to improve the physical performance of Olympic athletes by around 15%.[43]

Reactions to music are perhaps subjective, but a multitude of clinical studies reveal that cardiorespiratory variables are strongly influenced by music. Music has been found to have a positive influence on people suffering from depression; it has also been shown to reduce hypertension, improve sleep quality, lower blood pressure and improve respiratory volume.

So, what should we be playing? The University of Niš research team suggests that some genres of music are less effective such as heavy metal, which was found to raise stress levels. Classical music had a proportionately greater positive impact than any other genre, and the researchers identified that specific musical instruments, including the organ, piano, flute, guitar, harp and saxophone, were all effective at getting those endorphins flowing.

So, here are the top five tunes that have been scientifically proven to boost happiness and improve your wellbeing:[44]

- Bach's *Brandenburg Concerto No. 3*
- Verdi's *Va Pensiero*
- Puccini's *Turandot*
- Beethoven's *Symphony No. 9*
- Vivaldi's *Four Seasons*

It's time to pop another dime in the jukebox and bring the sound of music to your life.

17. OLD HABITS

If we want to perform at our best, then instilling great habits into our daily routine is key.

Let's face it, you're probably quite busy and, no doubt, there are considerable parts of your day already taken up with your daily routine – all those rituals we perform at an intuitive level every day, almost on autopilot.

This is entirely normal. The human brain is hardwired to work this way. It operates at a largely subconscious level.

Think of an iceberg, with only its tip above water. The top part is your conscious mind – the bit we like to think makes all the decisions. However, anyone who has ever had the sudden inexplicable urge to scoff some junk food – only to immediately afterwards wonder why they did it – understands that sometimes we make choices from somewhere else.

Our values and beliefs are stored within our subconscious. This is also the part of the brain that drives our habits, our routines and our rituals.

If you want to create new habits, the most difficult part is managing to stay consistent long enough for the habit to form. This takes sustained effort – typically around 28 days. If you're truly committed to creating a new behaviour, then you should start simply and easily – so that it's practically impossible to fail.

Where most people falter with new habits is that they start strong but then quickly fizzle out. However, if you incorporate something into your daily routine gently, you're more likely to maintain it.

So, if you want to do more exercise, then set a goal to do a one-minute workout a day. Or, if you want to drink less caffeine, try one cup as decaf, or drink the same number of cups of coffee but leave one unfinished.

If you've tried to form good habits before and failed, what went wrong? Did you start too strong? What were the barriers to your success?

_____

_____

_____

_____

_____

Successful habit formation requires just two things: the mental energy needed to commit to the new habit and an understanding of your own motivations.

18. TOUGH CALL

Look at your list of things to do today. Is there something there that you've been putting off?

Procrastination has become an art form for many people, but look deeper, reflect a little on those things you've been avoiding and you might just notice a pattern.

It's human nature to prefer completing the tasks we enjoy or find easy, nudging the tougher ones further down the priority list.

But today let's flip the game. Make the *toughest* call of the day first.

Look back at your to-do list. What's your toughest call this week?

It might be a call with someone you worry might give you bad news. Or a call to someone you have to give bad news to.

Your toughest call might even be an email requiring a detailed response, or preparing a slide deck for an important business meeting, or having a one-to-one conversation with someone.

Or it could be a meeting with someone you want to see but they seem to be avoiding you.

Here's the thing. These tasks won't be any less tough at 4pm this afternoon, after a good night's sleep or next week. In fact, it's the opposite: the low-level worry from the toughest call constantly lurks in the background of your brain, distracting you and making you less effective at everything else you're doing.

Right now, look back at your list. Identify your toughest call. And then just do it.

Sure, you may not *want* to. You may be telling yourself you have a plan. But crack on and make the call. It'll freshen the air, brighten your day and suddenly make your to-do list a whole lot lighter. It'll give your confidence a quick boost too, making it easier to tackle whatever's next, because you've made the toughest call first.

19. A SMASHING TIME

A study[45] by scientists at University College London reveals that being in a bad mood can actually be good for you. Apparently, mood swings serve a vital purpose in helping us adapt to changing situations.

When things are going well and we're in a good mood, we're more open to taking greater risks – and more likely to succeed.

When the chips are down, sulking helps to conserve energy and keeps our mind off taking chances.

But what about when it goes beyond a sulk? How about when someone really pisses us off and our blood starts to boil? What then?

Visiting Dallas, Texas, recently I was intrigued by the Anger Room, a sound-proofed place where I could really let off steam.

For a modest fee, it's possible to relieve stress by smashing stuff up, with no risk of upsetting anyone – or even having to clean up afterwards. The Total Demolition package comes with full protective gear, a lump hammer and a bunch of crockery to throw at the walls. A modest extra fee gets you a bucket of glass to throw, and if you want to go all out you can even have a mannequin made to look like anyone of your choosing. Of course, souvenir photos of you in full anger management mode are available to take home.

While the quick fix of throwing a wobbly may feel good at the time, we really do need to get to the bottom of our emotional response. It's thought that up to 60% of our anger can be 'unrectified anger' from our past, even as far back as childhood.[46]

Anger is, essentially, a primal defence emotion and can certainly be a way to express negative feelings. But it's also been shown to damage our health; after the 'letting rip' stage we need to find solutions to our problems. Talking things out with a therapist may help, but in the heat of the moment it's important to try to return to a state of relaxation as quickly as possible.

Professor Brad Bushman at Ohio State University reckons that counting to ten can be helpful – though he concedes that you may need to keep going to 20, 30 or even 100 in some cases!

If counting doesn't work, try Bushman's '3D' approach:

- **distraction** – deliberately focusing on something else, such as a book or song lyrics, to change your mental 'channel';
- **distance** – try to see yourself in the moment of anger as others do (take a fly-on-the-wall perspective);
- **display** – affection and aggression are incompatible responses; when we display one, it cancels the other out.

After the storm, it's useful to reassess the situation to understand why the anger response was generated. Could it be that we overreacted to something? Is there any concrete evidence that someone intentionally wanted to antagonize, hurt or humiliate us? Might we have misunderstood or assumed incorrectly?

MY THOUGHTS ON THE MIND

_____

_____

_____

_____

_____

_____

_____

_____

_____

_____

_____

_____

_____

_____

_____

_____

"The human body is the best picture of the human soul."

– Ludwig Wittgenstein

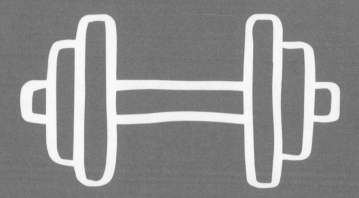

PART THREE

BODY

A WORD ON THE BODY

Your physical health is a major influence on your overall wellbeing. Yet, countless people continue to lead busy, stress-filled lives, paying little attention to their health and fitness.

Today, only around 10% of all jobs require physical effort. In contrast, just 50 years ago, nearly half of all jobs demanded some kind of huff and puff, sweat or elbow grease.

In the US, only 6% of all job roles meet the government's guidelines for physical effort at work.[47] Today, one in every three Americans are classified as obese, and a further third as overweight.[48] That's two in every three with a body weight issue – and, interestingly, it's the same proportion in the UK too.[49] By 2020, obesity-related disease will overtake smoking as the biggest killer of Americans and will swallow up more than 20% of healthcare spend.[50]

What does this all mean? Well, today, 5,479 people around the world will die of a disease caused by a sedentary lifestyle.[51] Yes, today. *We've got to move more.*

Many folks assume that focusing on their health will be time-consuming or will involve major upheaval in their lives. However, while it's true that the human body is an incredibly complex machine, keeping it in optimal physical condition is remarkably easy.

The body's needs are few:

- **Physical activity.** Spend some time each day doing something that elevates your heart rate. This doesn't need to involve a visit to the gym – it could be walking to work, doing vigorous household chores or making love (do this last one right and it's good news for your mind, body and soul).
- **Healthy food.** Vegetables and fruits in their natural state contain nutrients and fibre, which are crucial for keeping you energized.
- **Water.** Your body needs water every day to function properly. Coffee, tea, fizzy drinks and alcohol are dehydrating. You don't need to avoid these things entirely, just remember to keep your water intake topped up.
- **Sleep.** Your body requires around eight hours of sleep a night. However, the quality of your sleep will be greatly improved if you respect your circadian rhythms and maintain a regular sleep cycle.
- **Relaxation.** Often thought of as something with only mental benefits, relaxation also aids physical wellbeing. It releases tension that has built up in the muscles and reduces levels of the stress hormone cortisol within the body.

If you exercise daily, eat well, drink sufficient water, sleep properly and remember to relax, the benefits will soon become visible to those around you. As well as endowing you with a toned body and clearer skin, it will give you heightened focus, a more positive outlook and greater self-esteem.

But despite having lived with yours for a while now, chances are you may not *really* know your body.

From the age of 30, your body starts to change significantly. You lose one sixteenth of an inch (1.59mm) in height each year. This might not sound like a lot but, in practice, it causes your posture to change as your vertebrae contract, forcing your hips and knees to bend towards the ground. At the same time, your body loses water and your vital organs shrink. Oh, and the arches of your feet flatten out, causing you to lose those trimmed calf muscles you love.

As these changes ramp up, your body consumes around 12 calories fewer per day for each year of age over 30. Yet you more than likely didn't know that, and are continuing to shovel in food in the same quantities as before.

20. GRUNTING HIGH AND LOW

Russian tennis pro Maria Sharapova has won five Grand Slams and was regularly ranked in the sport's world top ten. Despite this, she may be best known for her powerful oral volleys while on court.

Recent research[52] showed that Sharapova's 'grunts' – as they have rather unfortunately become known – often measure more than 100 decibels, often to the annoyance of her opponents.

Some spectators have complained that these guttural shrieks should be officially outlawed. They believe that the sounds not only disrupt the game but are also used as a way of cheating by unscrupulous players – either by masking the sound of the racket striking the ball so their opponent can't judge its trajectory, or as a way of directly distracting their opponent by drawing their attention away from the ball.

So what's all the noise about?

The study by the University of Nebraska had ten professional tennis players (five male and five female) participate in a set of standardized practice sessions – one with grunting and the other without.

During the testing, participants wore portable metabolic units to measure oxygen consumption and their shots were measured with a radar gun. It emerged that the grunting increased the players' average serving velocity by 3.8% – and had no effect on their oxygen consumption.

Rather than just being a tactical way to confuse or distract your opponents, it seems grunting increases 'trunk stability' – the ability to maintain active control of your spinal and pelvic posture during dynamic loading and movement situations – and improves the power of your performance without exerting any additional energy.

Researchers believe that primitive vocalizations also trigger the body's in-built fight-or-flight response, and this pushes more energy to the muscle fibres – a hangover from our savage ancestors.

Try grunting today and unleash your innate raw power. Just don't do it on the bus or train to work.

21. LIVING THE DREAM

Despite progress in sleep science over the course of the past century, researchers still can't explain why we dream – or even say what function dreams are supposed to perform.

Dreams might aid memory by sifting through our daily experiences and cataloguing the useful ones. Or, perhaps, what we perceive as 'dreams' are just our confused sensory functions attempting to make sense of the brain's process of disposing of unnecessary information. Or, possibly, dreams are just a sort of built-in 'Netflix and chill' for tired grey matter.

Whatever the situation might be, sleep is hugely important. If you think about it from an evolutionary perspective, spending a third of each day lying around unconscious must have left our ancestors extremely vulnerable to attack, so the benefits of sleep palpably outweigh the risk. But it's not easy, as Friedrich Nietzsche pointed out: "No small art is it to sleep: it is necessary for that purpose to keep awake all day."[53]

Around one in three adults have a sleep-related issue at some point in their lives, and 15% of us are chronic insomniacs.[54] Anyone who has felt the effects of sleep deprivation will know that sleep is essential – not only mentally but physically. Nothing beats a good night's sleep for our feeling of wellbeing. Sleep re-energizes the body, clears the brain, regulates appetite, aids recall and assists in learning – this is the reason we often make better sense of problems after 'sleeping on it'.

Sleep also helps us to process and integrate our emotions. When we have not had enough sleep, we often become short-tempered and our ensuing stress causes other functions of our mind and body to suffer.

Most adults should get between six and nine hours of sleep every night, but factors such as anxiety, stress, grief, working irregular hours and living with young children often preclude this.

If you find sleep a struggle, there are a number of things that might help:

- **Snack on bananas**, which help your body to produce the sleep-regulating hormone melatonin. You can also snack on yogurt and almonds, which are high in tryptophan, an amino acid that causes drowsiness.
- **Wind down**, which is a critical (and often neglected) stage in preparing for bed. Relaxation exercises, such as light yoga stretches, will help to relax your muscles.
- **Ensure your bedroom is a relaxing environment** – a room filled with TVs, mobile phones and other noisy, light-emitting

devices will cut your production of melatonin and weaken your mind's association with your bedroom as 'the place for sleep'.

- **Sleep in darkness** – your body has evolved to sleep better in darkness. Even if you work nights and have to catch up on sleep during the day, try to replicate night-time conditions. Fit some thick curtains to keep out the light.

- **Block out noise** – if you live in a noisy or built-up area, try investing in double glazing or, for a cheaper option, use earplugs. Anthony Burgess, author of *A Clockwork Orange*, is reputed to have once joked: "Laugh and the world laughs with you, snore and you sleep alone." f you share a bed with a partner who snores – and you're sure you want to keep them – earplugs might be a good option.

22. STEPPING OUT

Many people – especially successful business people – often balk when it comes to terms such as 'mindfulness' and 'meditation'.

Perhaps this is understandable. If those people have never really engaged in such concepts, they probably seem unnecessary – even a distraction from the 'proper business' of the day.

If you're in a role where your decisions have an impact on the success of your company and the jobs of the people around you, it might seem neglectful not to devote all your time to thinking about the job in hand.

However, mindfulness practices can help you to deliver clarity of vision and hugely improve your decision-making skills – and, crucially, can be simply (and unobtrusively) incorporated into your working day.

Probably one of the most powerful 'under-the-radar' techniques for everyday meditation is 'mindful walking'.

Mindful walking is a form of meditation that you can do without needing extra time in your day.

Most of us do a lot of walking – even if we don't realize it. We may walk some distance to work, walk to and from meetings, stride around the office or perhaps take a pet pooch for walkies in the morning before we leave for work.

Many folks naturally use their time walking to mull things over – how they'll respond to a pressing email, what they might say in the morning meeting, how they might deal with the thorny issues of the day. But mindful walking involves clearing the mind of as much of this stuff as possible and simply focusing on the action of the body as it moves.

The point of mindful walking is to keep your mind in the present moment and allow you to find a place of refuge from the distractions of the day, rather than allowing your wandering mind to ramble on.

Our mental health is challenged when we allow ourselves to dwell on the negative events of the past or on what other people have done to us. Instead, we need to come to each moment with a clean slate – and *live life today*.

With practice, mindful walking will help you to focus your mind, strengthen your concentration and connect with the present moment.

Wherever you happen to go today, as you walk along, concentrate on the sensation of your body's movement. Centre your mind on the feeling of your feet as they make contact with the ground. If your busy mind struggles to remain focused on such a simple proposition, count your steps from one to ten, then repeat.

23. YOGA PANTS

In the west, yoga is largely regarded as a physical practice – but, more correctly, it should be thought of as a multi-tiered system of living.

In India, yogis (people who practise yoga) believe that if we balance our actions, 90% of life's problems will be resolved.

In yoga, the fourth of the eight 'limbs' of preparation is a concept known as pranayama – from *prana* meaning 'life force' and *ayama* meaning 'control'. It is a vital exercise in attaining a healthy body and mind – and in gaining higher states of consciousness.

According to pranayama, our breath is our life force – our 'spirit'. Naturally, if you were seated next to someone on a bus who told you that "your breath was your spirit", you'd probably get off at the next stop. However, this may not be as crazy as it seems – after all, the root of the word 'spirit' is *spiritus*, the Latin word for 'breath'. So really, by definition, when we regulate our breath, we are controlling our spirit.

Within pranayama, there are a number of different techniques to control the breath. Some activate your sympathetic nervous system – the human fight-or-flight response. However, these days, knowing how to trigger these reactions is largely unnecessary, as most people are living with inflated levels of stress much of the time anyway.

What are more usually taught in yoga classes are techniques designed to activate the parasympathetic nervous system, in order to aid rest and digestion.

Complacency often blinds people to the huge benefits of breathing effectively. Used properly, breathing exercises can be a great tool in improving mood, increasing mindfulness and keeping you performing optimally.

Here are a couple of helpful breathing exercises that can help to raise your spirit:

- Focus on breathing in and out through your nose, into and out from the stomach. Breathe lightly but deeply. This is a very effective technique in creating stress resilience.
- Take ten deep diaphragmatic breaths in through your nose and down to your abdominal region, allowing your stomach to inflate each time. As you increase the space in your chest cavity, you will give your lungs, rib cage and diaphragm more room to fill with air. Your heart rate will speed up on inhalation, and this will pump more blood to your muscles and raise your brain's alertness.

24. GET OUT!

The latest edition of the *Oxford Children's Dictionary* removed previously listed words including 'blackberry' (the fruit), 'canary', 'clover' and 'pasture' and included 'Apple' (the brand), 'attachment', 'blog' and 'BlackBerry' (the gadget).

Twenty years ago, 40% of children regularly played with friends outdoors. Today that number has plummeted to less than 10%.

According to the United States Environmental Protection Agency, the average American adult now spends 90% of their time indoors.[55] 'Nature deficit disorder' is fast becoming a thing as we rapidly lose our connection with the natural world.

Scientist Dr Selin Kesebir, of the Center for Healthy Minds at the University of Wisconsin–Madison, is concerned that indoor activities such as television, video games and the internet are "being substituted for nature as ... source[s] of joy, recreation and entertainment" and are partially to blame for the rise in mental ill-health around the world.[56]

Kesebir's studies reveal that being outside in nature reduces anxiety and stress, enhances creativity and increases our ability to relate to other people. "Connecting with nature is great for our wellbeing, mental health, and cognitive performance."

Even just looking at pictures of lakes and mountains leads to faster stress recovery, mental restoration and boosted brain power.

National Geographic adventurer, Alastair Humphreys, is a poster boy for wellbeing. Lean, alert, always smiling, chilled out and in the moment, he's cycled solo around the world, walked across southern India, rowed across the Atlantic Ocean, run six marathons through the Sahara Desert and completed a crossing of Iceland on foot. All this by a self-confessed "slightly weedy, unfit, wimpish person not ideally suited to a life of adventure and without the necessary skills".

Humphreys reckons that most folks don't take on such challenges because they think they don't have enough money or time, don't live somewhere geographically wild or exciting, don't have the right equipment, or are not fit enough.

He encourages people to take 'micro-adventures': deliberately small, almost provocatively mundane adventures. These micro-adventures are close to home and can be done on the weekend or even midweek.

On his website, Humphreys suggests leaving work at five o'clock, taking a train out of town, spending the night sleeping on a hill and being back at your desk by nine o'clock the next morning.[57]

In that brief moment, you've had a proper adventure: you've gained wilderness experience, you've done something you've never done before and you've challenged yourself.

Micro-adventures can be whatever you imagine. What will you do? How about:

- sleep in your garden – or a friend's if you live in an apartment;
- have brekkie in the woods – grab your flask and a croissant or bagel and just go;
- take a night walk – in town or country, letting the stars light your way;
- build a campfire on the beach – sausages or marshmallows on sticks get bonus points;
- swim in the wild – find a river, lake or ocean and dive right in.

25. FITNESS IS ANCIENT HISTORY

If you want to feel happier and healthier, the answer may not be running marathons or pumping iron but rather recognizing what your body is designed to do and adapting your lifestyle accordingly.

Natural selection shaped the human genome to succeed in the wild as a very active outdoor generalist. Indeed, for more than 90% of the time modern humans have existed on the planet, they have lived as hunter gatherers.

Long before there were gyms filled with personal trainers intoning blandly about 'personal bests' and 'going for the burn', humans were thriving just by living their everyday lives. We survived countless eons by foraging for nuts and berries and by chasing down animals to capture and eat.

In the developed world, however, modern culture has progressed in such a way that our lifestyles are now exactly the opposite of what we're designed for (prolonged periods of activity followed by intermittent rest).

Today, most people spend the majority of their time stationary – moving only very sporadically.

Add to our new-found sedentary lifestyles an abundance of easily available food completely unknown to our ancestors and our occasional drinking of enormous quantities of (alcoholic) liquids – without any intention of quenching a thirst – and it is little surprise that obesity is becoming a huge problem in the Western world.

So, without quitting our jobs and going back to live in the woods – or investing in Lycra and putting ourselves at the mercy of perma-tanned, chiselled fitness instructors – how might we go about making some positive changes to our lifestyles?

Well, the good news is that you don't really have to 'exercise' per se. Instead, simply up your level of daily activity. Adults should be active daily. Here are some guidelines on keeping fit:

- Over a week, your activity should add up to 150 minutes of moderately intensive movement – in ten-minute (or longer) bursts.
- Perform muscle-strengthening activities at least two days per week – this can be anything from pushing weights to cycling to dancing to hill walking.
- Incorporate balance and co-ordination exercises (such as squatting, standing on one leg or wall press-ups) at least two days per week.
- Try to minimize the time you sit down (get up and walk around a bit, or have a stretch).

Just do it.

Put this book down and spend the next ten minutes being active. Do some push-ups, sit-ups and star jumps. Go for a brisk walk. Or a spin on your bike. Go on – you'll feel great afterwards, and I'll be right here cheering you on from the sidelines.[58]

26. DRINK PROBLEMS

Many of us are trying to live healthier lives – but finding ways to do it that aren't boring can be tricky.

When it comes to healthy eating, you'll find inspiration for dishes that are 'healthy but taste great' in practically every newspaper.

While we're routinely informed about the ills of drinking too much caffeine and alcohol, there seems to be a paucity of ideas about what should replace them.

Water is obviously good for you, but it is hardly the most interesting drink – and, as such, is rarely considered a treat. So what are the alternatives?

The World Health Organization recommends that adults have less than 26g (6 teaspoons) of sugar a day, but a 500ml bottle of cola has around 53g of sugar (12 teaspoons). So, if we want to live healthily, clearly fizzy drinks are out.

Shop-bought coffees can be even worse. According to the details on its website, a well-known high-street coffee chain serves a flavour of Frappuccino containing a whopping 74g of sugar per serving. *That's more than 18 teaspoons of sugar.*

Surely, fruit juices must count as a healthy option though, right? Well, you need to check the labels. A lot of supermarket 'fruit juices' have very little to do with real juice. They contain either a small percentage of fruit or, in some cases, no actual fruit at all – just chemicals that make the drink taste a bit like fruit. What you're actually drinking is just fruit-flavoured sugar water – but putting that on the label probably wouldn't encourage sales.

Even fruit drinks or smoothies that do contain 100% juice are not that healthy. After all, all the good stuff from fruit – such as the fibre – has been taken out. What's left? Just the sugar.

These days, sports drinks have risen in popularity – and supermarkets are now crammed with various brands. However, these drinks were designed with athletes in mind and contain electrolytes (think 'salts' such as potassium, calcium and magnesium) and sugar. While these things can be helpful to athletes, most people going about their normal lives don't require additional salts, and they certainly have no need for liquid sugar.

Obviously, all these drinks are fine in moderation. But, if you want to stay healthy, water is essential. If you want to liven it up a bit, you could always buy some (non-caffeinated) herbal tea bags or sparkling mineral water.

At the end of the day, you wouldn't water your plants with a can of fizzy pop or a frothy cup of coffee, so you probably shouldn't water your insides with them either.

27. DON'T WASTE YOUR BREATH

Breathing is pretty much the first – and the last – thing we'll all do in life.

It's perhaps a little odd, then, that most adults aren't actually very good at it.

Though breathing is not usually considered a skill – indeed, it rarely features on even the most desperate job applications – it's a fact that, as most of us get older, we actually get a lot worse at it.

Most adults have forgotten how to breathe well – and the worst part is that, as we get bogged down in the minutiae of everyday life, very few of us think much about it at all.

Ask yourself, what do you do when you begin to feel yourself running low on energy or getting stressed? Drink a cup of coffee? Eat a chocolate bar?

But improving our breathing should be the first thing we do when it comes to increasing our energy levels and living well.

It's a major trope of every TV cop show to have a police detective checking a seemingly lifeless body to see whether the person is breathing. This makes sense, as respiration is the key vital sign in human beings. But just how *vital* is it? What is the true power of this thing we do unconsciously every second of every day of our lives?

Well, if done correctly, breathing helps with:

- releasing stress;
- reducing anxiety;
- stimulating the resting and digestive parts of your autonomic nervous system;
- aiding muscle relaxation;
- lowering blood pressure;
- boosting your immune system;
- triggering endorphin release and improving feelings of happiness and wellbeing;
- providing pain relief;
- stimulating the lymphatic drainage system of the body to remove toxins.

To breathe in the way that is best for your body, the inhaling needs to be done by the diaphragm so that your breathing is really deep. The air should come in through your nose and travel all the way down until you feel as if it is in the pit of your stomach.

Let's have a go at breathing together now:

1. Place one hand on your chest and the other on your belly.
2. Inhale deeply through your nose and into your belly – try to push the hand on your belly forward.

3. As you inhale count (in your head) 1, 2, 3 and up to where it's a comfortable challenge.
4. Exhale fully through your mouth, aiming for the exhale to take twice as long as the inhale (so, if you got to 4 on the inhale, aim for 8 on the exhale).
5. Repeat five times.

How are you feeling?

_____

_____

_____

_____

_____

_____

_____

_____

_____

_____

_____

_____

_____

28. BODY OF WATER

The human body can go for weeks without food but only about three days without water.

Water is massively important. It's not just that stuff you fill your kettle with, shower in or try to avoid buying bottled in overpriced restaurants – all life on planet Earth relies on it.

We are literally made of water. Our bodies are approximately 75% water: it makes up nearly 85% of our brain and about 90% of our blood.

Water also plays a vital role in practically every bodily function.

Around the globe, dehydration is the principal reason for day-time fatigue in adults. In fact, just a 2% drop in body water has a demonstrably negative effects on the brain and can produce a loss of short-term memory, problems with basic cognitive functions and difficulty focusing. To put this into perspective, lacking water is actually far worse for your brain than watching reality television!

In a properly hydrated body, the levels of oxygen in the blood-stream are much higher, and this means the body is more efficient at burning fat. The increased oxygen levels also give the body more energy. In addition, water is crucial for digestion and nutrient absorption – this is because carbohydrates and proteins are metabolized and transported by water in the bloodstream.

Thirst can often be mistaken for hunger. According to research carried out at the University of Washington, one glass of water killed off midnight hunger pangs for almost 100% of the dieters the researchers tested.[59]

There's one simple test that will tell you if you're not getting enough water. If your pee is colourless or pale yellow, you're probably fine. However, if your pee is any darker than that, you're most likely dehydrated and could probably do with drinking more water.

Why not try spending a week supplementing your usual intake of water by drinking two extra glasses a day and see how you feel? Even if you don't feel better, it'll probably improve your complexion. Which, thinking about it, will probably make you feel a bit better too!

29. FOOD FOR THOUGHT

It's a fact of modern life that, despite a greater emphasis on diet and nutrition, many people still eat badly.

For busy people, food is often an afterthought – something to be done on the move and squeezed in between meetings (or without even stopping work). This is not only bad news in terms of worker health but also often results in some seriously unpleasant computer keyboards.

Grazing on the hoof – while it might save a bit of time – is actually very bad for us, simply because the human body is not designed for the modern business world.

In evolutionary terms, humans are little more than a blink of an eye away from their cave-dwelling ancestors. Just because we've learnt how to use hair products and have traded in our furry loincloths for Calvin Kleins, doesn't mean our body functions have radically altered.

If we're stressed – as people often are at work, even if they don't realize it – our bodies are not expecting to eat. They're more likely gearing up for a fight-or-flight response – either in readiness for an angry confrontation with Ugg from the cave down the road or else to leg it from an itinerant mammoth.

Stress is part of the human body's defence against impending danger – and, traditionally, when humans are faced with imminent threats to their safety, breaking out sandwiches has rarely been the natural response. If it had been, it's unlikely the species would've made it quite as far.

It's not just the digestive system that is affected by stress either. It also steals energy from the brain, causing decision-making to become difficult.

Over a prolonged period, elevated levels of cortisol – the stress hormone – damage our physical, mental and emotional health. They also confuse the brain and cause it to make bad food choices. This is why when people are stressed they naturally reach for high-calorie 'comfort foods' such as chocolate and chips.

Whenever you eat, treat your food with respect. Give yourself a few minutes to remove yourself from the distractions around you, and ensure that you're taking your time and chewing slowly. This is important, because whenever we come into contact with food, either by taste or smell, the mouth starts to secrete saliva. Saliva contains enzymes that actively break down food, and its production also gives a signal to the stomach to start making way for digestion.

When eating is rushed, food isn't processed correctly and people continue to experience hunger pangs even when they're full – resulting in them eating a lot more than is necessary.

30. MOVE IT, MOVE IT!

Most people know that being physically active is good for the body – but fewer seem to be aware of just how closely linked their physical and mental health are.

The correlation is so clear that many doctors are now even recommending physical activity as a method for combatting growing rates of depression and anxiety – rather than the more conventional route of prescribing antidepressants.

Exercise will make you feel good (though, if you're a bit out of practice, it might not necessarily feel that way initially) due to the fact that when you take part in any form of physical activity, your brain releases endorphins – the 'feel-good' hormones – as a reward. This will naturally lift your mood and increase your feelings of wellbeing.

The more exercise you do, the less stress and tension you'll feel, due to the fact that ongoing exercise means your brain becomes more adept at controlling levels of the stress hormone cortisol.

When you feel stressed, which people often do after a hard day of work, it causes your body to produce adrenaline – the hormone that encourages that fight-or-flight response. This raises your heart rate, increases your blood pressure, sends blood to your muscles and gets you ready to put 'em up or make a dash. However, the natural high you experience from the endorphins released during exercise will counter those tense, edgy feelings and make you feel calm again.

A study[60] for the Economic and Social Research Council surveyed more than a million adults about their exercising habits. It discovered that, in the previous four weeks, 46% of people had not walked for 30 minutes continuously, 88% had not been swimming and 90% had not been to a gym. If you think you're not getting enough exercise, don't worry – you're hardly on your own.

So, whether you're feeling stressed or not, try taking a few positive steps in the right direction today – but start slowly, and build your fitness levels up over time. Don't try to run a marathon on day one.

Here are a few ideas that might help you to gently raise your game:

1. Take the stairs instead of the elevator.
2. Go for a stroll in your lunch hour.
3. Get off the bus a stop earlier and walk the final part of your journey.
4. Do some light exercises – such as stretching – before you leave for work in the morning.
5. If you work in an office, instead of phoning or emailing a colleague, walk over to their desk.

31. GIVE IT A REST

The famous American high-school philosopher Ferris Bueller once remarked: "Life moves pretty fast – if you don't stop and look around once in a while, you could miss it."

Many people spend long periods of their adult lives worrying that time is passing them by. That there just aren't enough hours in the day to get everything done. That they don't have time to meet friends, go to the gym, take a vacation or even take a lunch break. If this is you, don't worry – you're not alone.

Whatever speed you live your life, you're now operating at a pace unheard of even a generation ago.

Recent technological developments have accelerated our lives exponentially – yet, for all the innovations, our bodies haven't changed. They have slowly evolved to be perfectly in tune with the environment – but unfortunately, it's an environment we have systematically reshaped over a period of several thousand years – and our bodies haven't yet caught up.

Unlike modern technology, our bodies are generally easy to understand and to look after. Our 'operating system' is founded on very basic needs.

Ideally, it requires about six to nine hours of sleep a night, regular nutritious meals, sunlight, clean water, some physical activity, stimulating work and inspiring, loving relationships. That sounds pretty simple, right? But check back on that list – how many of them do you feel you are really, honestly achieving?

Of course, falling short of some of these needs is fine – and, in the short term, it won't do you any harm. Long term, though, it's another story. Adults who sleep fewer than six hours a night have a 13% higher mortality risk than those who get seven hours,[61] and they are 30% more likely to be obese.[62]

All the time it's helping you to work long hours, perform labour-intensive tasks and miss sleep, your body is eagerly waiting for you to stop – so that it can shut down and repair itself. So, if you're neglecting it – either by working it too hard or by allowing yourself to develop bad habits – you can be sure, sooner or later, there'll be a response.

In today's fast-paced world, your body has one requirement that outweighs all others – rest.

For us to continue to live active, mentally stimulating, sociable and healthy lives, the rules are simple: the more you challenge it, the more your body needs rest.

Here are a few things that will help you rest better:

- **Avoid caffeine and big dinners.** Many people will tell you of the benefits of 'switching to decaf' in the afternoon to aid restful nights. However, it's also important to steer clear of big meals late at night, as these stimulate your metabolism, which will wake you up. Try to have your last meal at least three hours before you hit the sack.
- **Forget the nightcap.** An alcoholic drink before bed might help you to drift off, but booze-induced sleep is usually poor quality and leads to disrupted nights.
- **Don't sleep in.** Yep, I know! Oddly enough, sleeping longer is not helpful. Though it will give your body a chance to repair itself, when you sleep for too long, your sleep is often fragmented and shallow. Nine or ten hours of fitful sleep is less useful than seven hours of good sleep.
- **Free your mind.** Make it a goal to always wind down before bedtime. Spend an hour doing something calming – read something, meditate, listen to soft music or take a warm bath.

32. THE BEAUTY OF SLEEP

The risks of high blood pressure, stroke, diabetes and heart disease have long been known to rise sharply in people who don't get enough sleep. However, more recent research has revealed that a lack of sleep is also linked to obesity.

Clearly, people who don't sleep well aren't lazier than people who do, so what is it that causes sleep-deprived people to put on weight?

The level of cortisol (a stress hormone frequently associated with weight gain) rises in people who don't sleep well. This activates receptors inside the brain that make us hungry. Sleeplessness is thus responsible for ruining many a good diet.

It seems that sleep deprivation impairs activity in the frontal lobe, so that the sleep-deprived lose the mental clarity to make good food choices. It's a little like being drunk. In fact, if the average person stays awake for 17 hours a day, this has the same effect on their reactions as drinking two glasses of wine.

When the body is overtired, the amygdala region of the brain engages and attempts to compensate for the lack of energy reserves in the body by creating cravings for high-calorie foods. This might go some way to explain sheepish-looking business-folks making late-night visits to kebab shops.

The human immune system is also reliant on regular sleep. When we miss a few decent nights' sleep, it struggles to defend the body against foreign or harmful substances. If the lack of sleep is ongoing, it can actually change the way the immune system responds: many sleep-deficient people are unable to fight off common infections.[63]

For most people, too little sleep is due to lifestyle choice rather than deeper psychological issues. So, if you're missing out due to late-night working or because you're binge-watching boxsets and can't tear yourself away, you should probably take note – missing sleep is habit-forming and isn't doing your general health (in both the short term and the long term) very much good.

Create a sleep schedule that suits you and try to stick to it – even at weekends. This will help to regulate your circadian rhythms (or 'body clock') and, in time, this will improve your quality of sleep.

33. WATER RUNS DEEP

Drinking water is crucial for the human body because it helps our cells to perform cellular respiration, take nutrients from our food, break them down and turn them into energy.

Water also aids digestion so, if you're constipated, it's far better for you to drink lots of water than take over-the-counter remedies.

As if that wasn't enough, water is also essential in regulating body temperature and assisting in cerebrospinal communications, and is vital in the transmission of hormones and signals across our bodies.

Water is also a critical component of our 'synovial fluid', which lubricates joints, allowing them to move smoothly so we don't experience pain.

Despite the myriad benefits of drinking water, around 90% of people are not getting nearly enough. But what exactly is the right amount?

Well, recommendations vary widely, but a good rule of thumb is:

Half your body weight in pounds = the amount of water you should drink in ounces.

A bit confusing? Not really. Especially if you're used to the US system.

What it means is that if you weigh 180lbs, then you should aim to drink 90 ounces a day. That's about 2.7 litres.

If you prefer measuring this in kilograms, then try:

0.033 × weight (kg)

For example, 180lb is around 82kg. So that would be 0.033 × 82 = 2.7 litres.

There are many environmental factors that influence how much water you need – from the temperature of the day to how much time you spend in an air-conditioned space. If you speak a lot as part of your job, you'll need to factor this in too. All that chat dries your mouth more quickly.

And, of course, how active you are has a bearing on how hydrated you'll need to keep. So if you're sweating more, drink a bit more.

When you drink the right amount of water, not only will your overall health improve but you'll also see improvements in your alertness, focus, energy and, yes, even skin clarity.

How much water should you be drinking? Work it out now:

0.033 × your weight in kilograms:

_____ *kg =* _____ *litres of water per day*

or

Your weight in pounds:

_____ *lbs divided by 2 =* _____ *ounces per day*

34. HOW TO LIVE FOREVER

The medical journal *The Lancet* reports[64] that around half of all babies born in industrialized nations since 2010 can expect to live into triple digits.

You may have heard that residents of Okinawa Prefecture in Japan commonly live to be 100 years old. Okinawa has the highest proportion of centenarians in the world, four times more than anywhere else. Japan has led the longevity charts for years, with an average life expectancy in 2015 of 83.7.[65]

In second place is Switzerland with an average age at death of 83.4. At the end of 2015 there were 1,562 centenarians living in that country.

The UK ranks 20th with an average life expectancy of 81.2 years.

Wherever we are, we're living longer than ever. However, thanks to the removal of the default retirement age and the miniscule state pension, over 15% of British men are still in employment at age 70 (up from 10% in 2012) while the number of women in work at age 70 doubled between 2012 and 2016.[66]

Around the world we see retirement age edging upwards. If you plan to retire at 65, things will be markedly different for you if your life expectancy is 100 compared to 80. We need a new perspective on how we plan for old age.

Anatomist Gabriele Zerbi wrote the first guide to long life – *Gerontocomia* – in the late 15th century. For people to live long and prosper, he advised plenty of fresh air, eating viper meat and a potion made from distilled human blood, ground up rocks and gold dust.

Certainly, nutrition is important. Vegetarians often appear to live healthier and longer lives than omnivores. It's worth considering what Okinawans – those folks amongst the longest living on the planet – eat; their diet is rich in vegetables, seaweed and fish. Many Okinawans practise *hara hachi bu* (literally 'eight parts out of ten full'), which refers to eating until sated but never stuffed.

In the 1980s, in *How to Live to be 100 or More: The Ultimate Diet, Sex and Exercise Book*, George Burns explains his secrets: wake early and begin the day with 45 minutes of floor exercises (sit-ups, push-ups and stretches) and then take a brisk 15-minute walk around the neighbourhood. These exercises gave Burns enviable muscle tone and may have contributed to his longevity, as may the fact that he took a nap every day at 3.30pm. His bestseller was penned at the ripe old age of 87, and, in case you're wondering, he did indeed make it to the goal he set himself in the title of his book.

Scientists are keen to understand the keys to invincibility and, increasingly, as we learn to control and manipulate the genes involved in the ageing process, "the possibilities of lengthening life appear practically unlimited" (so says William Regelson, professor of medicine at Virginia Commonwealth University).[67]

Dr Harrison Bloom, senior associate at the International Longevity Center in New York, concurs, although he clarifies that this "would assume better eating habits, a healthier lifestyle and continuing improvements in the environment."[68]

So, what to do?

Eating less certainly seems to be a remarkably easy way to live longer. According to scientific research, we can live up to 50% longer lives by cutting our consumption. Dropping our daily calories by 20% can extend our lifespan by a couple of years, while regular fasting may stretch things by up to a decade or more.[69]

Studies on rats show a 40% lower calorie diet enables the animals to live 30% longer,[70] while monkeys consuming 30% less calories each day for periods of up to 15 years live longer and avoid many age-related diseases.[71]

Lab tests show that fruit flies dosed with resveratrol (an antioxidant in red wine) live remarkably longer than other flies. The sirtuins (types of protein involved in regulating cellular processes including ageing and cellular resistance to stress) in resveratrol have been found to block calorific take-up and slow the ageing process in mammals. This restriction in calories triggers the release of fat stored in the body and sends the message that it's time to switch to survival mode. So the occasional glass really could be good for you. Cheers to that!

In the book *The Thing About Life Is That One Day You'll Be Dead*, David Shields pulls a lot of the advice on this subject together. Shields reckons that if you want to live longer, you should:

> Move to the country, not take work home, do what you enjoy, feel good about yourself, get a pet, learn to relax, live in the moment, laugh, listen to music, sleep at least six hours per night, get married, hold hands, have sex regularly, have lots of children, get on well with your parents, accept your lot in life, stimulate your brain, learn new things, be optimistic, don't smoke, do eat dark chocolate, drink red wine and green tea, eat a diet of fruit, vegetables, olive oil, fish and poultry, exercise regularly, have clear life goals, take risks, have close friends, don't be afraid to seek psychological counselling, be a volunteer, have a role in the community, attend church, believe in something.

It's quite a list. How many do you do?

My great Aunt Sylvia lived to 95. She was a woman of elegant simplicity, and a week before her death I asked what her secret to a long and happy life was. "Whisky every day," she announced – though, after hearing her explanation (a teaspoonfull in her tea each morning), I wasn't quite so thrilled.

MY THOUGHTS ON THE BODY

_____

_____

_____

_____

_____

_____

_____

_____

_____

_____

_____

_____

_____

_____

_____

_____

"Follow your soul. It knows the way."

– Anon

PART FOUR

SOUL

A WORD ON THE SOUL

Oxford Living Dictionaries will tell you that 'soul' is:

1. The spiritual or immaterial part of a human being or animal, regarded as immortal.
2. Emotional or intellectual energy or intensity, especially as revealed in a work of art or an artistic performance.

When discussing the human soul, it can be difficult to talk in specific terms or with any degree of clarity. However, presumably because its existence has been considered self-evident for eons by countless civilizations and religions, the concept still retains weight.

Certainly, if you were to approach someone in the street and ask them what they consider to be 'good for the soul', they would almost certainly propose things that they believe to be beneficial at an abstract or spiritual level.

A common idea is that 'crying is good for the soul' simply because so many people repress their feelings. Raw emotions are often covered up – out of politeness or embarrassment, maybe – and, without a proper outlet, sadness and grief can build to become significant stress and anger. Venting emotions releases our tensions and brings about an apparently soul-deep feeling of catharsis.

Another seemingly innocuous activity often posited as having powerful, long-term effects on the soul is being positive. Research shows that maintaining an optimistic outlook has been linked to everything from reducing feelings of loneliness to increasing pain tolerance.

Meditation is also oft-considered beneficial to the soul. By emptying the mind completely and staying focused on the moment, practitioners are reminded that they are not simply a mind but are, instead, a human soul full of thoughts, feelings and experiences. Meditation helps us to attain a state of serenity and brings mental and physical healing to the body.

Laughter is most regularly considered to be the true salve for the soul, because it relieves stress and triggers the release of endorphins, the body's natural 'feel-good' chemicals. This promotes an overall sense of contentedness and wellbeing. Hey, have I told you the one about the nun, the priest and the camel?

These days, anything that purports to make us feel deeply satisfied can be prefixed with the word 'soul' – including food, music and art.

Most things deemed 'good for the soul' are also those that bring enrichment to both body and mind – and this is unlikely to be coincidental.

There are now hundreds and perhaps thousands of books sold on knitting, brewing beer and even stacking wood.[72] For many of us in this busy world, there's a growing desire to get back to basics, be more authentic, find peace and escape the din of the world around us.

Of course, there's something slow, sustainable and meditative about these kinds of pursuits. My own love of chopping wood bears this out. Chopping. Sorting. Stacking. Burning. The 'four heats of good wood', as my nonagenarian neighbour says. A roaring fire stoked by gentle satisfaction.

As Erling Kagge points out in his splendid little book *Silence,*[73] activities that are good for the soul are:

> a profound human need. You set yourself a goal and carry it out, not all at once, but over time. You use your hands or your body to create something...the results you achieve are not things that can simply be printed out. The fruit of your labour is a tangible product. A result that you and others can enjoy over a period of time.

So, are you ready?

Let's get it on.

35. CURIOUS BRAIN

One of my earliest memories is a gift my Aunt Beryl gave me. It was a stuffed toy: a chocolate brown monkey called George.

I was perhaps four or five years old.

When I pulled a string from George's back, a recorded voice would ask me questions such as: "How are you?", "What's your name?" and "What do you like to do?"

Even though I quickly memorized the sequence of questions George would ask me, this never stopped me replying, as me and my monkey chatted happily. George was cool. He was my friend.

Everyone who types something into Google's search bar and hits 'enter' is curious about something. And we do this 2.4 million times a minute, every minute of every day. I've done the math for you – that's nearly 3.5 billion searches every day around the world.

In *A Curious Mind*,[74] Brian Grazer reckons that curiosity is, "the spark that starts a flirtation – in a bar, at a party, across the lecture hall.

And curiosity nourishes the romance, and all of the best human relationships – marriages, friendships, the bond between parent and child."

It's the curiosity inside that makes us ask a simple question like:

- How are you?
- How was your day?
- How are you feeling?
- What have you been up to?

And it's curiosity that then prompts us to listen to the answer and prepare to ask the next question.

As Grazer points out: "Curiosity can add zest to your life, and it can enrich your whole sense of security, confidence and wellbeing."

If you're bored in a business meeting, curiosity can save you.

If you're fed up with your career, curiosity can rescue you.

If you're angry, curiosity can help you channel the frustration constructively.

If you're scared, curiosity can give you courage.

If you're feeling uncreative or unmotivated, curiosity can be the cure.

Psychologists define curiosity as 'wanting to know'. It starts out as an urge, a simplistic desire, but then becomes more active, more searching: a question. Zoologist Paul Meglitsch said that: "...nearly every great discovery in science comes as a result of providing a new question rather than a new answer."[75]

As adults, sadly, we defer our questions to Google. For kids it's much more pressing and intriguing. Even when presented with a cuddly fake monkey called George.

But curiosity isn't just a means to understand the world – it's a way of changing it.

In a letter to his biographer, Carl Seeling, in 1952, Albert Einstein remarked that: "I have no special talents. I am only passionately curious."

Try as I might, there are only two things that I haven't been able to find on the internet nowadays:

- the answer to a question that hasn't already been asked;
- a new idea.

The internet, as fantastic as it is, can only tell us what we *already know*.

Consider your own experiences – at work and at home. What should become clear is that authentic human connection is founded on curiosity. To be a good boss, you have to be curious about those who work with you. To be a good partner, you have to be (and stay) curious about the other person. To be a good parent, a good friend or a good colleague, you'll need to be curious too.

Grazer created what he called 'curiosity conversations', which he used to get close to people who intrigued him or with whom he wanted to connect. Each started the same way: "I've always been curious about your work. I'm trying to broaden my sense of that subject, would you be willing to spend 20 minutes talking to me about what you do, what the challenges and satisfactions are?"

Whether you're looking to move on up in the world, produce blockbusters or simply get a little more excitement into your life, you'd do well to follow Grazer's approach:

1. Make it clear you want to hear the other person's story.
2. Prepare what you'd like to get out of the conversation. Plan a handful of open questions such as: "What was your first success?", "Why did you decide to do what you do?" or "Tell me about a big challenge you've had to overcome."
3. Stay flexible: don't stick rigidly to your question set. Ask, listen, ask more questions. The goal is to keep learning.
4. Be respectful of time.
5. Show gratitude for the time shared.

As Einstein is quoted as having said in *LIFE* magazine in 1955: "The important thing is to not stop questioning. Curiosity has its own reason for existing."

Oh, and there's a double bonus: curiosity is democratic. And it's free. You don't need a special training course. Or protective clothing. Or high-tech equipment, a smartphone or a high-speed internet connection. You've already got everything you need: you were *born curious*. Just ask!

36. LISTEN UP

If we truly care about the relationships in our lives, we must listen mindfully.

Have you ever been introduced to someone and then within a few minutes of being told that person's name suddenly realized that you have no idea what it is? This is surprisingly common and, in most instances, has nothing to do with bad memory. The new name probably didn't get as far as your memory in the first place.

Our brains often fail to absorb details simply because we are too busy thinking ahead to what we might say next – in an effort to avoid the possibility of an awkward silence.

Our fear of these awkward moments is natural – no one wants to look boring or dull-witted, especially at the start of a relationship or encounter. Consequently, learning to listen mindfully in such circumstances can feel like a tricky thing to pull off – but, really, it just takes a little practice.

Think about a teacher, lecturer or leader who has inspired you in your life. What was it that made the difference?

It's likely that you appreciated that they demonstrated a genuine interest in what you thought or what you had to say – and, in doing so, made you feel valued.

The next time you speak to someone, instead of showing you're engaged by looking for gaps in the conversation to inject intelligent responses, take a mental step back.

Look into the person's eyes as they talk. This will help them to retain their focus and allow you to disassociate yourself from distractions around you. Take a deep breath and make the effort to actively listen to what they're saying.

You'll likely find that, when you reply, your responses are more honest, measured and relevant, and that your overall sense of 'connection' is radically enhanced.

After time, mindful listening becomes second nature and you'll find yourself not only hearing the words more clearly but also able to feel the emotions behind them. This will help you to build much stronger relationships and people will naturally be drawn to talk with you as an excellent listener.

37. GOOD TO BE GOOD

The world's mood often seems to fluctuate depending on the economic pressures of the day.

When the global financial crisis hit in 2007, it was closely followed by a distinct attitude shift. Politics suddenly became less tolerant and quick to blame, and many people seemed unable to see beyond their own personal situation.

It sometimes feels as though our collective generosity of spirit is more linked to the money in our pockets than to the 'content of our characters', to paraphrase Martin Luther King.

Following the crisis, recorded feelings of wellbeing slumped across the world – and not just because the population at large felt let down, angry or scared. It was also because performing kind and selfless acts – one of the most powerful ways of enhancing personal wellbeing – dropped off as everyone felt more than a little dismayed.

Naturally, it feels good when you hit your own goals – getting that dream job, gaining a new qualification or just enjoying a well-deserved vacation – but your overall sense of wellbeing is much more enhanced when you do things for other people.

Research for the American Psychological Association has proved that committing 'random acts of kindness' can vastly improve our levels of personal contentment. When we perform a selfless act, oxytocin – the 'love hormone' – is released into the brain, boosting our feelings of optimism and self-esteem.[76]

A study at Yale University found that performing acts of kindness improves your capacity for dealing with stress. According to the report,[77] the ongoing flood of oxytocin forms a protective barrier against the negative effects that stress can have on our mindsets.

A little bit of altruism in our daily lives can have an enormous impact on our sense of wellbeing. It doesn't have to be something like saving an orphan from a burning building – it can be as simple as donating a can of beans to a food bank, popping in for a cuppa with an elderly neighbour, putting some change in a parking meter that's running out of time or getting out of your chair on public transport to allow a pregnant or elderly person to sit down.

As John Ruskin is reputed to have remarked: "A little thought and kindness are often worth much more than a great deal of money." Once you start proactively looking for ways to exhibit kindness, you'll find there is no scarcity of opportunity and you'll quickly feel good as a result of the experience of doing good.

Today, your challenge is to find three opportunities to do something nice and get that oxytocin flowing. Ready? Crack on then!

38. LIVING IN FEAR

In 2014 I was invited to give a talk at an event organized by the TED organization.[78] They'd picked up that there was some crazy dude living on Lake Geneva who swam with great white sharks and figured he might make interesting listening.

But the sharks were only half of the story.

You see, ever since I was a kid, I've been afraid of the water. Lakes, rivers, swimming pools, even the bath tub – I was never a fan. Memories of childhood camping trips – with our parents encouraging my sister and me to go and play in a freezing Scottish mountain lochan – still make me shudder. Decades later, living *avec mes pieds dans l'eau*[79] as they say here along the coastline of the lovely Lac Léman, I'm still to beat the fear.

A fear of water is unusual. But many people have a fear of sharks – often as a result of *that movie*.

Not me, though. Water is quite enough to set my heart racing. Each time I don my wetsuit, my brain spirals out of control, imagining all the things that could go wrong: my air tank exploding, my breathing apparatus failing, me sinking to the bottom of the ocean. The 'what ifs', I call them.

Despite the human race nowadays enjoying unprecedented levels of safety and comfort, a 'culture of fear' is promoted in order for us to cope with the uncertainty and change we face in our lives. Under the cloak of anxiety, modern society advocates hesitancy and over-precaution as virtuous rationales for inaction. The 'what ifs' are a constant part of life as we know it today.

You see, the busier we are with our lives, the narrower our paths become as we choose comfort over challenge. As the negative thoughts swim around in our heads, our minds try to help us avoid worry by trimming down the list of potential things for us to do. Those 'what ifs' are powerful filters.

It's taken me the best part of 20 years to understand Mark Twain's view that courage isn't the absence of fear but the mastery of it. My approach isn't complex – I simply revise those 'What if?' questions to 'What if I could?' and let my mind go wild thinking about infinite possibilities rather than problems. In this way, I've slowly evolved my fear in order to get me incredibly close to the ocean's apex predators, reframing my perspectives on risk and harnessing the *power* of my fears. This has provided me with some of the most invigorating interactions of my life.

So, what are you afraid of? Susan Jeffers had a point in her book *Feel the Fear and Do It Anyway*.[80] Jump out of a plane, get close to spiders, learn to scuba dive. What would you do – if you could?

_____

_____

_____

_____

_____

_____

_____

_____

_____

_____

_____

_____

_____

39. I'M GONNA BE ...

As you might have gathered from the previous chapter, I love sharks.

So, when my nephew Charlie – then aged eight – asked me to come and speak about them to him and his classmates, I had to say "Yes!"

Having spoken in front of audiences including CEOs and top teams of Fortune 500 corporations, and on the TED Talk stage, I should have found this a walk in the park, right? Wrong. Kids are a different kind of audience. You can't speak *to* them, only *with* them.

Whereas adult audiences have been amazed at my intimate inter-actions with the world's most notorious 'man-eaters', this group of thirty kids, whilst captivated, treated my stories of sharing the seas with five-metre great whites as if it were as normal as kicking a ball around in the playground at break time.

At the end of the talk, I asked who might like to go swimming with sharks. All hands shot up.

The watery theme continued as one child told me of his plan to be a deep-sea diver searching for treasure on shipwrecks, and another a fishing boat captain chasing huge crabs in freezing oceans. A timid girl spoke of her intention to be a water-skiing champion. They were so excited about their futures. Nothing was impossible for them. They were all so excited about their dreams and totally convinced of their ability to be remarkable. Others shared their ideas about becoming an astronaut, a doctor saving lives in Africa and a top athlete representing their country. They believed not that 'anything is possible' but that 'nothing is impossible' – a much wider scope.

We can all be remarkable. It's simply that we forget this as we grow up.

As we age we fall into the trap of judgment: quickly rating and ranking what's remarkable and what isn't. In our urgent quest for the next big thing, we engage with and then cast aside activities and experiences as if they were little more than yesterday's news.

As I returned home from my shark talk, I pondered my visions for my own future. Some days later, in the attic, I discovered a box containing old school jotters. Leafing through them, I found a page titled "My Future" and read on with interest. At the same age as Charlie, I had written "I'm going to be a stuntman".

While today I may not be leaping from helicopters, dodging bullets or hopping through hoops of fire, I do often feel that I'm out there on the edge – *living* life.

In his superb book *The Monk and the Riddle*,[81] Randy Komisar suggests that the most dangerous risk of all is: "spending your life not doing what you want on the bet you can buy yourself the freedom to do it later".

We all have a choice – to simply exist or to live a truly remarkable life. So what do you choose? How will you be remarkable today?

40. AN ISLAND OF YOUR OWN

Sitting on a long-haul flight a while ago, I got chatting to my neighbour. We were heading back to Europe from the Middle East, both travelling for business. Over a glass of wine we swapped the usual stories of work, hotels and the challenge of local taxis finding the right destination.

We traded countries visited – first the top three, and then those experiences we'd rather forget. For fun I asked where she'd like to go but hadn't yet been.

"Fiji," was the answer. "Because with over 300 islands there I could surely find one for myself." The idea of solitude – a bit of peace and quiet – is something most of us yearn for from time to time. As the world around us gets busier and busier, and the lines between work and home life blur, it's natural to want to retreat to a place that's just for us.

"I'll never go, though," my neighbour added. "It's just too far away. It takes too long to get there. And I just don't have the time."

For 20 years now, my father has been reading the same book, *An Island to Oneself*.[82] In it, the author shares the story of his life on a desert island, deep in the South Pacific Ocean – indeed, not far from Fiji. Tom Neale, a 50-something New Zealander at the time, spent several years alone on Suvarov, a remote atoll in the Cook Islands. Dad reads the book three or four times a year, and has bought several copies to loan out to friends over the years – each become enthralled and the books usually fail to return. Dad just smiles and begins his search for a replacement, knowing he's ignited something.

Eleven years ago, to celebrate his 65th birthday, I arranged a trip to take Dad to Suvarov. It wasn't easy: a bunch of flights from Scotland to finally reach Samoa, a quick pilgrimage to the house where the Chief Adventurer – and fellow Scot – Robert Louis Stevenson lived, before boarding a rusting old bucket to cast off for the island.

After four days of high seas (and the accompanying incurable sickness), just before 4am, with the sun peeling from its ocean bed, the first birds appeared. An hour later we could make out images of palm trees in the distance. Two hours later we stepped ashore.

For three days, we slept on board the boat and rowed to the white sand each morning, where we lazed beneath palms and feasted on coconuts, breadfruit, crab the size of dinner plates and fresh fish plucked from the sea with a bare hook.

On day four, our final night moored at Suvarov, a couple of hours after Dad had fallen into his slumber, the mate readied the dinghy and I packed the bag. After I woke Dad just sufficiently to guide him from his bunk to the rubber boat, we zipped over.

The next day, we awoke to glorious sunshine pouring through a worn, empty window frame dressed with a raggedy sack-cloth curtain. We were in Tom Neale's hut. His old maps pasted to the walls, his books rotting on the shelves. For one night, we had an island to ourselves. We were *there*.

It would be tempting to think that it was the pristine beaches, the fresh exotic fruits and the perfect blue sea that made this trip. But in fact, as Dad and I often recount the tales together, we know deep within us that it was the *adventure* itself that made this trip so memorable. Yes, really – it was the hours of travel, the state of our boat, the constant seasickness, having our fish ripped from our fishing lines by sharks, the pilgrimage to Neale's island, the perseverance and the time it took to find a way. Those moments, just father and son, together. *That* made this paradise.

Where is your paradise, your island? And what do you need to do to get there, even if just for one night?

41. REALLY HUNGRY CATERPILLARS

Today I watched in awe as a bright green caterpillar devoured a cabbage leaf in my garden.

It systematically gnawed away, creating patterns that left the leaf as an intricate skeleton reminiscent of the finest lace.

Back in the 19th century, French botanist Jean-Henri Fabre conducted a fascinating experiment in his garden in Provence. Fabre took a flower pot and carefully placed several 'processionary caterpillars' (as the name suggests, these little guys like to follow each other in lines) in single file around the circumference of the pot's rim.

Fabre dropped a handful of pine needles (the caterpillars' favourite food) into the middle of the pot. The caterpillars aimlessly followed each another until they reached full circle and found their own scent, and then paused, clearly confused. Fabre then wiped the rim of the pot and the caterpillars began their march again.

Almost eight days later, the caterpillars dropped dead of exhaustion and starvation. Yet nourishment was just inches away. Fabre was astonished: "I was expecting too much of them when I accorded them that faint gleam of intelligence which the tribulations of a distressful stomach ought to have aroused."[83]

Although I'm not aware of any caterpillar making a claim for superior intelligence, whether hungry or not, as humans, we are not too dissimilar to the processionary caterpillar. How often we navigate through life, going with the flow, following those just ahead of us, confusing activity with productivity.

After a period in such a procession, we may not die a physical death like the caterpillar. However, spiritual death certainly may arrive. Have you ever felt like you're going round in circles?

Our satisfaction with life is a key component of our wellbeing. Aimlessly shuffling forward in the hope of success or reward is, as for the caterpillars, circular. If we want to live a fulfilling life, setting goals is key.

So, before Fabre steps in and wipes the rim of your life with his cloth, have a think about what you're striving for.

What are the tribulations your "distressful stomach ought to have aroused"? What are you hungry for in life? Happiness comes to those who are making steady progress towards or achieving meaningful goals.

So your task now is to identify three clear goals. Ready?

1. Family goal:

_____

_____

_____

2. Work goal:

_____

_____

_____

3. Life goal:

_____

_____

_____

Now you have these goals, in which direction must you march to turn them into reality?

_____

_____

_____

42. WHAT HAPPENS IN VAGUS

The vagus nerve is the principal component of the human body's parasympathetic nervous system.

When you are happy and relaxed, it sends messages to your body to switch on your rest-and-digest mode and turn off your stress-related fight-or-flight mechanism.

Researchers have discovered that having a high 'vagal tone'[84] is directly linked to an individual's ability to experience positive emotions and increase positive social connections.[85] However, it also shows that social connections increase vagal tone – thus, creating a sort of self-perpetuating positive cycle that improves physical and mental health.

Studies by the New Economics Foundation[86] and NHS England[87] confirm that social connectivity has significant positive effects on wellbeing. But this doesn't mean that we all need to become social butterflies to be happy – we simply need to better manage the types of social relationships we engage in.

Having three or more good friendships is enough to guard you against most psychological disorders – but these friendships need to be with people who are supportive and encouraging.

A friend who constantly moans about their own problems and never wants to hear what's going on in your life is unlikely to have a positive impact on you at a physical or psychological level. Nor is a person who fires backhanded compliments at you or seeks to belittle you in front of others.

Think about the loyal friends in your life and learn to treasure them – love and support, especially unconditional love and support, should be valued. It doesn't take much skill to cultivate a close human bond, but it does take some effort – and it can help you lead a happier, healthier and more fulfilled life.

43. LIFE IS A
BLANK PAGE

Please Turn Over ➔

LIFE IS A BLANK PAGE

Blank pages terrify writers. They're more intimidating than the toughest critic, more depressing than the worst prose, more worrying than an overdue deadline.

I've had my share of concerns in writing this little book for you.

Fifty chapters seems a reasonable endeavour, and off I go, motoring along. Until, suddenly, it all dries up. Writer's block sets in, and the blank page stares back at me.

This morning, though, I seek wisdom in Anne Lamott's *Bird by Bird: Some Instructions on Writing and Life*. I'm buoyed by a snippet of text that reminds me that: "everything we need in order to tell our stories in a reasonable and exciting way already exists in each of us. Everything you need is in your head and memories, in all that your senses provide, in all that you've seen and thought and absorbed."[88]

Research suggests that free-writing (the act of getting thoughts down on paper) helps us to think more clearly. So, today, let your mind wander. Reflect on your own story. Lamott encourages us to: "take the attitude of what you are thinking and feeling is valuable stuff, and then be naïve enough to get it all down on paper".[89]

So, flip back to that blank page and start scribbling. Jot down your thoughts and feelings. Listen to your inner voice.

As Lamott says, when you: "stop trying to control your mind so much, you'll have intuitive hunches".[90]

I wonder what yours will be.

44. THE HAPPINESS ADVANTAGE

Studies consistently show that we rate our wellbeing as the most important thing in our lives – more important than success or income, and often even ranking above family ties and personal connections.

Despite what we may initially expect, wellbeing is not directly related to status, level of income, education, gender or race. So, the young admin assistant cycling to work in their old tennis shoes may be as happy as the executive driving to the office in their top-of-the-range car.

The pursuit of happiness fascinates psychologists as much as it intrigues media journalists, Hollywood film makers and society at large.

Research suggests that we may be born 'happy' – inheriting up to 50% of our cheerfulness and our subjective wellbeing from our parents. According to studies, we are all born with a certain level of happiness, known as the 'hedonic set-point'. Fortunately, for most of us, our set-points are usually above zero – i.e. on the happy side of neutral.

Around 10% of our happiness is circumstantial – where we live, what we earn, etc., and a whopping 40% comes from intentional activities – *the things we choose to do*.

In a study[91] of more than 2,300 individuals, social psychologists David Lykken and Auke Tellegan at the University of Minnesota, USA, found that almost 90% rated themselves as having high levels of subjective wellbeing *and* long-term happiness. It could well be, then, that as we human beings evolved, those of our forebears who were grouchy or miserable fared less well in the struggle for survival and had less luck in the mating game. This idea led the researchers to suggest that humankind has evolved a bias towards positive wellbeing simply through the process of natural selection.

Having what positive psychologists call the 'happiness advantage', or an optimistic, positive mindset, has been shown to help doctors improve the speed and accuracy of diagnosis by almost 20%,[92] raise the hit-rate of salespeople by over 37%,[93] increase the pro-ductivity and job satisfaction of office workers by more than 30%,[94] boost creativity[95] and build resilience.[96]

There's another thing, too, that affects our happiness. Whether you're feeling good or tend to see the glass as half empty, the research points to one thing above all else that boosts happiness time and again: gratitude.

Having an attitude of gratitude – simply recognizing and being thankful for things in our life – has reliably been shown to boost levels of dopamine in our brains, generating feelings of being alive and outwardly exhibiting signs of happiness.

Try identifying five things that you are grateful for in your life right now. Perhaps an old friend who's always there for you, a fancy dinner out, a delicious home-cooked meal, your stable job, a loving family, the fact that it's a sunny day ... what are you grateful for?

1. _____

_____

2. _____

_____

3. _____

_____

4. _____

_____

5. _____

_____

Just as with any other habit, in order to rewire our brain and gain the happiness advantage, we need to stick with this new approach for at least 28 days.

So, grab a notebook and place it by your bed or coffee maker, or somewhere you'll see it each day. Take a few moments every day for the next four weeks to record what you're grateful for. In just 28 days' time, your actions will have turned into habits and helped to maintain those elevated dopamine levels, bringing smiles to your face and happiness to your heart.

45. CONNECT THE DOTS

My friend Dave is a superstar on LinkedIn. His profile boasts thousands of connections from all walks of life and from right around the world. Many of them he hardly knows.

Dave accepts requests to connect from everyone, and he diligently sends invitations out to everyone who crosses his path – speakers he hears at a conference, new colleagues at work, encounters on his train ride to work.

University of Houston research professor Brené Brown reckons that "connection is why we're here".[97] She's right. Humans are social animals – we need to be around people, feel part of a tribe.

But human connection requires *trust*.

Real connection relies on *sincerity*.

And these connections grow through *compassion*.

Steve Jobs remarked that: "You can't connect the dots looking forward – you can only connect them looking backwards. So you have to trust that the dots will somehow connect in your future. You have to trust in something – your gut, destiny, life, karma, whatever."[98]

Brian Grazer is one of the most successful film producers in Hollywood. With productions such as *Splash, Apollo 13, A Beautiful Mind, 8 Mile* and *The Da Vinci Code* under his belt, it's likely that you've enjoyed his work. But what has been the key to his success?

Connection.

Starting out as a junior filing clerk but with grand dreams of becoming an award-winning movie producer, Grazer created a personal rule for himself. He had to meet one new person in the entertainment business every day.

Today, at age 67, Grazer still sticks to this rule, proving Steve Jobs right. Over the years, Grazer's connections have included A-list actors, media moguls, pop stars, royalty and even American presidents. These connections have opened doors and helped him to create some of the most memorable Hollywood blockbusters. They've helped him make his dreams a reality.

So how about applying Grazer's rule to your life right now? Imagine committing to meeting one new person – in your industry sector, an area you'd like to work in or a domain you're interested in – every day, for the next six months. You don't need to have deep and meaningful conversations that last for hours – just meet them and chat for five minutes. You could even do it over the phone or on social media (although Grazer always meets people in person).

Fast forward to six months from now and you'll know 180 people in your own field of work whom you don't know right now. Let's say that only 10% of these people have something to offer – a new perspective, some technical expertise, a bright idea. That'll still be an incredible 18 new allies on your side.

Grazer's rule underlines the point that to connect the dots, you first have to collect the dots.

It's something my mate Dave understands well. Maybe I should introduce you.

46. MISSION: INTUITION

It can be difficult being 'the boss'. Not only do you have worries about revenue, costs, staffing and the ever-evolving marketplace to contend with but also, whenever there are decisions to be made, you are expected to know exactly what to do.

There are huge stresses involved in constantly making the correct decision – often there are just too many variables to make a wholly informed choice. At the same time, most leaders know that it could be disastrous to show hesitation or weakness in front of shareholders, peers or employees.

It's lonely at the top and without anyone to call on for support – many leaders find themselves feeling isolated. Often, the uncertainty and fear of making a bad choice will create a suffocating mix of stress and anxiety that leaves them juddering to a standstill.

More experienced leaders – including Branson, Gates, Jobs and Mandela – choose a different route: they listen to that little voice inside their own heads called 'intuition'.

Whatever you're doing in life, whenever you try to find the answers from a place of logic, you may find yourself getting stuck. Problems lurch through your mind, pulling you in all directions. A more effective technique is often simply to relax and tune into your own intuition.

Our intuition – or 'source intelligence' – lies deep inside us. Rather than dismissing it as illogical nonsense, see it as an 'inner voice' – an instinctual feeling from within that tells us how we feel beneath our analytical thinking.

Most successful business leaders believe that the secret of their success lies behind having the courage to, as Steve Jobs said,[99] follow their "heart and intuition". With intuition, instead of agonizing over problems or trying to out-think yourself, you let go and allow yourself to be guided by what comes to mind.

If you've never put much stock in the power of intuition, start to pay attention to your inner thoughts and see what happens. New opportunities will present themselves – and you'll find yourself able to make quick decisions that you don't feel the need to second guess.

47. NETWORK SUPPORT

Strong relationships with people around us have a huge impact on our mental and physical wellbeing and our ability to deal with challenges in life.

Isolation and loneliness, on the other hand, are significant factors in triggering anxiety and depression and, surprisingly, can also have terrible negative repercussions on our physical health – on a par with smoking and obesity.

We may argue with the people we interact with socially – that's to say our partners, friends, family and work colleagues – or occasionally feel pressured and frustrated by them, but this is neither unusual nor unhealthy. It's entirely normal within the cut and thrust of any relationship.

In supportive relationships, we tend to share problems and, whether consciously or unconsciously, use the people around us as 'sounding boards' – a technique that helps us to keep things in perspective and allows us to make better judgments.

Knowing that support is available increases our feelings of personal security and self-esteem – and, of course, there is a pleasure in simply knowing you are in the company of people who want to be around you. Even at Christmas.

We often take relationships for granted when we're in the middle of them – and, when many of our daily interactions are taken up by discussions about washing up or taking out the trash, it's perhaps easy to see why – but supportive relationships add significantly to the quality of our lives.

The huge correlation[100] between people who experience mental health issues – such as anxiety or depression – and people who have experienced a loss of social connection or deterioration in the quality of their relationships is no coincidence.

Cherish your supportive relationships. At a functional level, your entire outlook and way of life are based on them – whether you realize it or not.

Spend a day just thinking about the important relationships in your life and take a moment to reflect on how they enrich you. Now think about what life would be like if they weren't there.

Would your life still have the same sense of meaning and purpose?

Right!

So when will you make time for them this week? Next week? And from now on?

48. MOUNTAIN HIGH

Before the 19th century, mountains were deemed vast, impenetrable parts of the landscape whose looming, unknowable peaks touched the heavens.

Around the middle of that century, mountaineering became fashionable – not only as a sport but also as an exercise in derring-do. A way for young men to test their mettle by facing the adventure of the unknown.

When the English mountaineer Edward Whymper overcame death to successfully navigate to the peak of the Matterhorn in 1865, he was justly regarded as a hero.

Heroes always need adversity, and mountains have always been thrilling locations because their conditions are extreme – and, as such, safety is not guaranteed.

George Mallory's famous quip about scaling Mount Everest simply "because it's there" actually says little about why scores of mountaineers are drawn to the sport. For many, the act of climbing mountains is less about physical conquest and more about making a journey of self-discovery.

While statements such as 'no risk, no reward' often come across as clichéd, it's a fact that most experienced mountaineers consider the risk involved as being intrinsic to the experience. It's the vividness of feeling offered by the empty solitude of the mountain, as the mountaineer clings to its walls, that provides the rush that keeps them coming back for more.

The risk forms the heart of the experience – an intoxicating sense of freedom that, within the same instant, forces the mountaineer to live in the moment and to overcome their sense of self.

How we face adversity in our lives is a vital step towards self-realization. When we face extreme situations, will we turn back in panic? Or will we find the strength to carry on?

You might not be climbing a mountain today, but there is a lesson that we can all learn here. Rather than taking the path of least resistance, to truly experience life and understand who we are as people, we sometimes need to step outside our comfort zones and face our fears.

As the poet T S Eliot once said: "Only those who will risk going too far can possibly find out how far one can go."

49. IT ALL DEPENDS ON US

In an interconnected world, the challenges of communication grow daily. Effective communication is no longer just a matter of language – it now spans the vastness of products and services in our lives, and the interplay of attitudes, beliefs and cultures too.

Whether at work or at home, in established relationships or new ones, we all struggle to be heard, to make our point, to encourage action or to really connect with another person from time to time.

Well, all of us except Sir David Attenborough. When I was watching the final episode of his BBC television show *Blue Planet II*, I nearly fell from my seat when he looked me straight in the eye and said: "The future of all life now depends on us."

With images of plastic waste filling the oceans – birds mistakenly feeding their young slivers of the stuff, a deformed turtle trapped inside a plastic wrapping, mother dolphins weaning their calves on toxic milk and a whale with a plastic bucket stuck in its mouth – it was hard not to feel the force of his words. I felt certain he was talking to *me*. So, I vowed immediately to stop using single-use plastics – such as takeaway coffee stirrers and plastic bags – and have switched to taking a refillable water bottle on my business trips.[101]

Over years of watching and reading works by Attenborough, I've come to learn that his successful approach hinges on his audience doing three things:

1. **Understanding** (what he says). There is a famous saying that you can only really explain something when you understand it fully yourself. Another way of looking at this is the idea that we should speak so that eight-year-olds understand our message.[102] So, break it down, and use analogy, bold images and simple words – just like Attenborough does so well.
2. **Agreeing** (with his point). The only way for this to happen is for the recipient of your message to understand what's in it for them. What connects them to what you have to say? Clarify and emphasize your point with meaningful facts. While people understand logic, we connect more strongly through emotions. That's why Attenborough's call to arms was so persuasive. When he tells us – on *Blue Planet II* - that two in every three of the fluffy young chicks we watch on screen will die within days, it's much more impactful than if he'd said that only 33% will survive.
3. **Feeling** (compelled to act). In the busy world in which we live, there's always something we need to do. Our lists grow by the day! So, if you want someone to do something, make it clear. Don't provide a list of suggestions – point clearly to the action you'd like to see. Just like Sir David does.

Attenborough changed the way the world thinks about plastics. Within minutes of *Blue Planet II*'s final episode airing, social media was alight with personal pledges and calls for lawmakers, governments and commercial corporations to shape up.

The great man was right – it really is up to us, and we *all* know it.

50. DEAD END

If you've ever employed the services of a personal trainer, you might be forgiven for thinking that they were some kind of superhero. And, let's face it, all those Lycra-clad muscles probably helped to skew your perceptions a bit.

The thing is, though, that even in the case of the most physically fit and health-conscious people, hidden somewhere beneath all that sinewy, well-toned flesh there is a human being – and, sadly, like the rest of us, one day they must inevitably die.

Ultimately, we're all going to croak one day – and, in the grand scheme of things, it really doesn't matter how many bench presses you do, how many miles you log on the treadmill, or how many kale and ginger smoothies you pour down your neck. At some point – hopefully in the far-distant future – your body will shut down and you will breathe your last.

When it comes to death, really the best we can ask for is that we aren't doing anything too embarrassing at the time.

The irritating part of the whole death 'deal' is that we can never really say when it will happen. However, it makes sense to do what you can to keep healthy each day, if only in an effort to delay the inevitable.

Elizabeth Bowes-Lyon, The Queen Mother – a symbol of strength for Britain during the dark days of the Second World War and an icon into the new millennium – lived to be 101. What was her secret? Attitude.

"Wouldn't it be terrible if you'd spent all your life doing everything you were supposed to do?" she once said. "Didn't drink, didn't smoke, didn't eat things, took lots of exercise, all the things you didn't want to do, and suddenly one day you were run over by a big red bus, and as the wheels were crunching into you you'd say: 'Oh my god, I could have got so drunk last night!' That's the way you should live your life, as if tomorrow you'll be run over by a big red bus."

Knowing that we will ultimately die, we really should try – in the midst of all the calorie counting and gym visits – to occasionally remember to live.

We all only have one shot at life, so we need to make the most of it and live now. We're a long time dead, so take a moment each day to feel the blood coursing through your veins and realize what a privilege it is just to be alive. Once in a while, we all need to remember to let our hair down, kick off our gym shoes, raise a glass, smile and just enjoy the feeling of being here.

When the day does come, and your life is flashing before your eyes, try to make sure you've got something extraordinary to watch.

Create a quick 'bucket list': jot down five things you'd love to do but never have. They can be as audacious as you wish, such as 'do a naked parachute jump', or more low-key, such as 'climb a tree'.

1. _____

_____

2. _____

_____

3. _____

_____

4. _____

_____

5. _____

_____

_____

OK, first part done. Now decide to do one of them today. Yes, *today*.

I know you're wondering whether you really should crack on and do this thing, so let's end with the words of 1980s chat show genius Clive James: "Stop worrying – nobody gets out of this world alive."

MY THOUGHTS ON THE SOUL

_____

_____

_____

_____

_____

_____

_____

_____

_____

_____

_____

_____

_____

_____

_____

_____

IN CLOSING

All right, you made it. Well done!

Now, take a moment. Think back on what you've been reading here. What you've been doing. How you've been feeling.

Breathe deeply ...

... and have a go at answering these questions. Rate your responses on a scale of one (low) to five (high).

1. How *well* do you feel right now?

2. How *happy* have you felt over the past 30 days?

3. Do you feel you have *meaning* in your life?

4. Do you feel you have sufficient *emotional and social support* in your life?

5. How *satisfied* are you with your life nowadays?

Flip back to the little exercise you did in Chapter 1: 'What Exactly is Wellbeing?' How do your answers now compare? Why do you think that is? What's changed in you? Where do you want to focus your attention *now*?

_____

_____

_____

_____

_____

_____

_____

FIFTY-PLUS

Right back at the start of this book, we took the World Health Organization definition of 'health' to be the "state of complete physical, mental, and social well-being and not merely the absence of disease or infirmity".[103]

I've suggested that 'wellbeing' is how *happy, contented, comfortable* and *satisfied* we are in our lives and how effectively we *function*. But keep in mind that it's all about you, so however you define your wellbeing is totally cool. Really.

We've explored 50 ways to *master your mind, boost your body* and *supercharge your soul* in a bid to beat dysthymia[104] and help you to recharge your batteries. I sincerely hope that you've found some useful ideas in these pages.

Of course, 50 ideas can be a lot, so what is it that we all *really* need to be doing? Well, if you want a little more *oomph*, a bit more *buzz* and a dash more *dynamism* then I reckon there are five things you can focus on. Here they are:

1. **The triple R.** *Relax, rest, recharge* (and a fourth if you fancy it: *repeat*). We're putting our bodies through too much. Make sure you give yours time to bounce back.
2. **Breathe the pressure.** It's psychosomatic. So, inhale, inhale! Exhale, EXHALE! You gotta focus on better breathing. Down into the belly – get the nose and the mouth working.
3. **Move it!** Sitting for more than four hours is killing you.[105] No, really it is.
4. **You are what you eat.** And drink. Put the good stuff in, get the good stuff out.

5. **Habits.** No messing around, now's the time to start. If you swear too much, drink too many or smoke like a haystack, don't despair: bad habits can be cured by cutting them out. And slot in some good ones from this book.

IT'S NOT OVER YET

OK, now find one of those plastic or fabric one-metre tape measures and a pair of scissors.

Cut it at your age – for me it's 44.

Now cut it again at your probable age at death – family history and a quick appraisal of your current lifestyle should help you here. Be brave. For me, I'm guessing 88 years. So now I have a tape that reads 44 at one end and 88 at the other.

Now, this is what you've got left (so, that's 44 years for me).

And you're going to spend a third of this time sleeping.[106]

It's time to wake up.

TO LIVING

The Roman philosopher Seneca said that, "life is very short and anxious for those who forget the past, neglect the present and fear the future". But, "life is long if you know how to use it".[107]

As we discussed right back at the beginning of this book, 'wellbeing' is a subjective term. Now that you've worked through these pages, what does it mean to you?

_____

_____

_____

_____

_____

_____

_____

I really hope that this wee book helps you to bring just a bit more happiness, contentedness, comfort and satisfaction into your life.

Why?

Because you deserve it.

Now listen: if you remember only one thing from this book, remember this: you're a human *being*, not just a human *doing*.

Carpe Diem. Seize the day. Tide and time wait for no-one.

REFERENCES

1. OK, they are experiments, but I'm genuinely interested in how these people are feeling too!

2. Ala Alwan (ed.), *Global Status Report on Noncommunicable Diseases* (Geneva: World Health Organization, 2011), Chapter 1.

3. Tracy R. G. Gladstone, William R. Beardslee and Erin E. O'Connor, "The Prevention of Adolescent Depression," *Psychiatric Clinics of North America* 34(1) (2009): 35–52.

4. Alwan, *Global Status Report*, Chapter 1.

5. Luke Allen, "Are We Facing a Noncommunicable Disease Pandemic?" *Journal of Epidemiology and Global Health* 7(1) (2017): 5–9.

6. "Constitution of WHO: Principles" (World Health Organization, 1948), accessed 2 August 2018, http://www.who.int/about/mission/en.

7. The World Health Organization estimates that 300 million people worldwide could now suffer depression – the leading cause of disability worldwide. It's always a smart idea to check in with your doctor if you're feeling any kind of depression. This can take a bit of courage, though. If you're feeling under a black cloud, take a deep breath and book an appointment – the fact that you're reading this book already proves you're keen on making things better for yourself.

8. Ed Diener tends to be able to pull things together pretty neatly. His book *Assessing Well-Being* condenses all of his thinking and explores the ideas of others, and it is a great place to go for further reading. See Ed Diener (ed.), *Assessing Well-Being: The Collected Works of Ed Diener* (Dordrecht: Springer, 2009).

9. Variants of these questions were recently added to the UK Office of National Statistics's surveys as part of a governmental push to create a new UK Happiness Index.

10. Simon Sinek, *Start with Why: How Great Leaders Inspire Everyone to Take Action* (London: Penguin, 2009).

11. Simon Sinek, "How Great Leaders Inspire Action" (TED, 2009), accessed 2 August 2018, https://www.ted.com/talks/simon_sinek_how_great_leaders_inspire_action.

12. *Thriving at Work: The Stevenson / Farmer Review of Mental Health and Employers* (London: Department for Work and Pensions, 2017), 5.

13. "Mind Culture" (Institute of Leadership & Management), last modified 27 September 2017, https://www.institutelm.com/resourceLibrary/mind-culture.html.

14. David Cameron, "General Well-Being Speech" (20 July 2006), accessed 2 August 2018, https://conservative-speeches.sayit.mysociety.org/speech/600012.

15. David Adam, *The Man Who Couldn't Stop* (London: Picador, 2014), ##.

16. Carlo Cavagna, "Interview: Anthony Hopkins," About Film (2006), accessed 2 August 2018, http://www.aboutfilm.com/movies/w/worldsfastestindian/hopkins.htm.

17. Matthew A. Killingsworth and Daniel T. Gilbert, "A Wandering Mind Is an Unhappy Mind," *Science* 330 (6006) (2010): 932.

18. Killingsworth and Gilbert, "A Wandering Mind." For a summary of the study, check out Steve Bradt, "Wandering Mind Not a Happy Mind," *Harvard Gazette* (11 November 2010), accessed 2 August 2018, https://news.harvard.edu/gazette/story/2010/11/wandering-mind-not-a-happy-mind.

19. Herbert A Simon, Designing Organizations for an Information-Rich World in M Greenberger (Ed.) Computers, Communications and the Public Interest. Baltimore, MD: The John Hopkins Press, 1971.

20. See this excellent little guide for some great tips on looking after your mental health with mindfulness: https://www.mentalhealth.org.uk/sites/default/files/How%20to...mindfulness.pdf

21. Britta K. Hölzel, James Carmody, Mark Vangel, Christina Congleton, Sita M. Yerramsetti, Tim Gard and Sara W. Lazac, "Mindfulness Practice Leads to Increases in Regional Brain Gray Matter Density," *Psychiatry Research* 191(1) (2011): 36–43.

22. Kevin McSpadden, "You Now Have a Shorter Attention Span than a Goldfish," *TIME* (14 May 2015), accessed 2 August 2018, http://time.com/3858309/attention-spans-goldfish.

23. https://www.washingtonpost.com/blogs/erik-wemple/wp/2014/05/12/associated-press-polices-story-length/?noredirect=on&utm_term=.0000806b1ed9

24. *Attention Spans* (Consumer Insights, Microsoft Canada, 2015), accessed 2 August 2018, https://www.scribd.com/document/265348695/Microsoft-Attention-Spans-Research-Report.

25. http://news.bbc.co.uk/2/hi/science/nature/1834682.stm

26. https://www.huffingtonpost.com/entry/mind-wandering-creativity-mental-illness_us_5818acc4e4b0990edc33827a

27. Don't worry, it's just treehouses, huts, shacks, sheds and lodges – all clean and above board.

28. Erling Kagge, *Silence in the Age of Noise* (London: Penguin, 2017), ##.

29. Suzuki, S., *Zen Mind, Beginner's Mind: Informal Talks on Zen Meditation and Practice*. (Shambhala, Boulder, Colorado, 2006).

30. David R. Francis, "What Reduced Crime in New York City," *NBER Digest* (January 2003), accessed 2 August 2018, http://www.nber.org/digest/jan03/w9061.html.

31. http://www.post-gazette.com/business/businessnews/2012/05/13/Habitual-excellence-The-workplace-according-to-Paul-O-Neill/stories/201205130249

32. Dr Alexi Gugushvili keynote address to the British Sociological Association's annual conference, 10th April 2018, Newcastle-upon-Tyne, United Kingdom.

33. Nielsen, 2016. The Nielsen Comparable Metrics Report. The Comparable Metrics Series, Q2 2016.

34. Have a look at this *Business Insider* report to get you going: https://www.businessinsider.com/1-in-3-people-check-smartphones-night-deloitte-study-2016-9. Deloitte are really into research on smartphone use, check out their *'There's no place like phone'* report for a solid overview that reflects 53,000 people across 31 countries and five continentsr: http://www.deloitte.co.uk/mobileuk/?_ga=2.96460188.1636225352.1534004692-1821299274.1534004692

35. Aitken M., *The Cyber Effect: An Expert in Cyberpsychology Explains How Technology Is Shaping Our Children, Our Behavior, and Our Values – and What We Can Do About It*. (New York, Spiegel & Grau, 2017).

36. https://www.moneytalksnews.com/survey-one-third-americans-choose-cell-phone-over-sex/

37. This is pretty straightforward: just go to the 'rules' settings in your mail system. Ask your computer to move all messages that contain (for example) 'unsubscribe'. I promise you'll thank me!

38. Michiko Kakutani, "Transcript: President Obama on What Books Mean to Him," *New York Times* (16 January 2017), accessed 2 August 2018, https://www.nytimes.com/2017/01/16/books/transcript-president-obama-on-what-books-mean-to-him.html.

39. See Eammons RA, *Gratitude Works!* (San Franciso, Jossey-Bass, 2013) for details of the study and some fantastic discussion.

40. Check out Chapter 20 – 'Grunting High and Low' – to see. Maria is waiting.

41. Gilbert's original research is contained in Gilbert D, Wilson TD, Pinel EC, Blumberg SJ and Wheatley P. 1998. "Immune Neglect: A source of durability bias in affecting forecasting". *Journal of Personality & Social Psychology*, 75(3), 617-638. An easier (and happier) read is in his book *Stumbling on Happiness*, (New York: Vintage, 2007).

42. M. Deljanin Ilic, S. Ilic, R. Pavlovic, G. Kocic, D. Kalimanovska Ostric, V. Stoickov, D. Simonovic and V. Ilic, "Effects of Music Therapy on Endothelial Function in Patients with Coronary Artery Disease Participating in Rehabilitation," *European Heart Journal* 34 (2013): 5797, accessed 2 August 2018, doi:10.1093/eurheartj/eht310.P5797.

43. Hans-Joachim Trappe, "Music and Clinical Health," paper delivered to the ESC Congress, 27–31 August 2011.

44. Luciano Bernardi, Cesare Porta, Gaia Casucci, Rossella Balsamo, Nicolò F. Bernardi, Roberto Fogari and Peter Sleight, "Dynamic Interactions Between Musical, Cardiovascular, and Cerebral Rhythms in Humans," *Circulation* 119 (2009): 3171–3180.

45. Eldar E, Rutledge RB, Dolan RJ, Niv Y. 2016. "Mood as representation of momentum". *Trends in Cognitive Science*, 20(1), 15-24.

46. See, e.g. the Mental Health Foundation (2008) report *Boiling Point* at http://www.mindyouranger.com/wp-content/uploads/pdf/documents/boiling-point-report.pdf

47. https://health.gov/dietaryguidelines/2015/guidelines/appendix-1/

48. https://www.cdc.gov/obesity/data/adult.html

49. Public Health England, 2018. *Adult Obesity Trends*.

50. Centers for Disease Control, 2018. *National Health Highlights Report*.

51. See e.g. http://www.who.int/mediacentre/news/releases/release23/en/ for more on the obesity crisis

52. Callison ER, Berg KE and Slivka DR. 2014. *Grunting in tennis increases ball velocity but not oxygen cost*. Journal of Strength and Conditioning Research 28(7) 1915-1919.

53. Friedrich Nietzsche, *Thus Spake Zarathustra* (University of Adelaide, 2016), accessed 2 August 2018, https://ebooks.adelaide.edu.au/n/nietzsche/friedrich/n67a/chapter2.html.

54. https://www.cdc.gov/media/releases/2016/p0215-enough-sleep.html

55. Google The National Human Activity Pattern Survey (NHAPS) to find out more or find the full report here: https://indoor.lbl.gov/sites/all/files/lbnl-47713.pdf

56. https://centerhealthyminds.org/news/a-blow-to-well-being-nature-words-disappearing-from-books-films-and-songs

57. See www.alastairhumphreys.com.

58. Alright, here's a sneaky hack: I love doing 'one-minute workouts'. Find an excuse to get away from your desk for a minute – like nipping to the loo, for example – and just pump out some moves for 60 seconds. My favourites are push-ups, tricep dips and star jumps. Shhhh! Don't tell anyone!

59. Reported at: https://www.yeshealth.com/why-we-should-all-drink-more-water/

60. Farrell L, Hollingsworth B, Propper C and Shields MA. *The socioeconomic gradient in physical inactivity in England*. The Centre for Market and Public Organisation, University of Bristol. Working Paper 13/311, July 2013.

61. Robert Adams, Sarah Appleton, Anne Taylor, Doug McEvoy and Nick Antic, *Report to the Sleep Health Foundation: 2016 Sleep Health Survey of Australian Adults* (Adelaide Institute for Sleep Health, 2016). https://www.sleephealthfoundation.org.au/pdfs/surveys/SleepHealthFoundation-Survey.pdf.

62. Kristen L. Knutson and Eve van Cauter, "Associations between Sleep Loss and Increased Risk of Obesity and Diabetes," *Annals of the New York Academy of Sciences* 1129 (2008): 287–304.

63. Adams et al., *Report to the Sleep Health Foundation*.

64. *The Lancet*, 392 (10146) 451-530.

65. Compare life expectancies at: https://countryeconomy.com/demography/life-expectancy

66. See https://www.bbc.com/news/business-39344000

67. Noted in David Shields, *The Thing About Life Is That One Day You'll be Dead*, (New York: Alfred A Knopf) page 182.

68. Reported at: https://abcnews.go.com/Health/WellnessNews/half-todays-babies-expected-live-past-100/story?id=8724273

69. Richard Weindruch and Rajindar S. Sohal, "Caloric Intake and Aging," *New England Journal of Medicine* 337(14) (1997): 986–994.

70. William R. Swindell, "Dietary Restriction in Rats and Mice: A Meta-analysis and Review of the Evidence for Genotype-Dependent Effects on Lifespan," *Ageing Research Reviews* 11(2) (2012): 254–270.

71. John R. Speakman and Catherine Hambly, "Starving for Life: What Animal Studies Can and Cannot Tell Us about the Use of Caloric Restriction to Prolong Human Lifespan," *Journal of Nutrition* 137(4): 1078–1086.

72. Check out the best-seller *Norwegian Wood* by Lars Mytting (London: MacLehose Press, 2015); it's a side-*splitting* read that moves with a *chop* and will leave you *burning* with desire.

73. Kagge E., *Silence: In the age of noise* (New York: Penguin Random House, 2017).

74. Grazer, B., *A Curious Mind* (New York: Simon & Schuster, 2015).

75. Quoted in Marks EA, 2002. *Business Darwinism: Evolve or Dissolve: Adaptive Strategies for the Information Age* (New York: Wiley 2002). Page 99.

76. Fredrickson, B. L., Cohn, M. A., Coffey, K. A., Pek, J., & Finkel, S. M. (2008). "Open hearts build lives: Positive emotions, induced through loving-kindness meditation, build consequential personal resources". *Journal of Personality and Social Psychology*, 95, 1045–1062.

77. Raposa, EB, Laws HB & Ansell EB. (2015). "Prosocial behaviour mitigates the negative effects of stress in everyday life". *Clinical Psychological Science*. 4(4), 691-698.

78. The speech referred to was organized by TEDx in Lausanne, Switzerland, on 24 February 2014. You can find a video of the talk on YouTube: https://www.youtube.com/watch?v=B7-DQFvD5ck. Take a look if you're interested in the method I use to get my fears under control – or if you like sharks.

79. Literally 'with my feet in the water'; in reality, 'living close to the lake'.

80. Susan Jeffers, *Feel the Fear and Do It Anyway* (New York: Random House, 1987).

81. Komisar, R., *The Monk and the Riddle: The Art of Creating a Life While Making a Living*. (Cambridge, MA: Harvard Business Review Press 2001).

82. Tom Neale, *An Island to Oneself* (London: Collins, 1966). This chapter is dedicated to Neale – a man of courage and hardiness who wasn't afraid to be brave. The book is no longer in print but you may manage to find an old copy at flea markets or an old book shop if you look carefully. Your persistence will be well rewarded if you do.

83. Fabre, JH, *The Life of the Caterpillar*, (New York: Dodd, Mead & Company, 1916) Page 77.

84. 'Vagal tone' is essentially the activity of the vagus nerve, a fundamental component of the parasympathetic branch of the autonomic nervous system. When vagal tone increases (and sympathetic tone decreases), heart rate decreases.

85. L. Muhtadie, M. Akinola, K. Koslov and W. Berry Mendes, "Vagal Flexibility: A Physiological Predictor of Social Sensitivity," *Journal of Personality and Social Psychology* 109(1) (2015): 106–120.

86. Anna Coote, "Building a New Social Commons" (New Economics Foundation), last modified 2 May 2017, https://neweconomics.org/2017/05/building-new-social-commons.

87. Nicola Kay, "Health as a Social Movement" (NHS England), last modified 4 May 2018, https://www.england.nhs.uk/blog/health-as-a-social-movement.

88. Lamott, A., *Bird by Bird: Some Instructions on Writing and Life* (New York: Anchor. 1995) Page 181.

89. Ibid. page 113.

90. Ibid. page 113.

91. Lykken D and Tallegen. 1996. "Happiness is a Stochastic Phenomenon". *Psychological Science* 7(3) 186-189.

92. Carlos A. Estrada, Alice M. Isen and Mark J. Young, "Positive Affect Facilitates Integration of Information and Decreases Anchoring in Reasoning among Physicians," *Organizational Behavior and Human Decision Processes* 72(1) (1997): 117–135.

93. Sonja Lyubomirsky and Kennon M. Sheldon, "Pursuing Happiness: The Architecture of Sustainable Change," *Review of General Psychology* 9(2) (2005): 111–131.

94. Jennifer L. Sparr and Sabine Sonnentag, "Feedback Environment and Well-Being at Work: The Mediating Role of Personal Control and Feelings of Helplessness," *European Journal of Work and Organizational Psychology* 17 (2008): 388–412.

95. Carlos A. Estrada, Alice M. Isen and Mark J. Young, "Positive Affect Facilitates Integration of Information and Decreases Anchoring in Reasoning among Physicians," *Organizational Behavior and Human Decision Processes* 72(1) (1997): 117–135.

96. Matthew J. Grawitch, David C. Munz, Erin K. Elliott and Adam Mathis, "Promoting Creativity in Temporary Problem-Solving Groups: The Effects of Positive Mood and Autonomy in Problem Definition on Idea-Generating Performance," *Group Dynamics: Theory, Research, and Practice* 7(3) (2003): 200–213.

97. See Brown's excellent TED talk at: https://www.youtube.com/watch?v=X4Qm9cGRub0&feature=player_embedded

98. Jobs uttered these words during his address to students at Stanford in 2005. You can read the full speech here: https://news.stanford.edu/2005/06/14/jobs-061505/

99. https://news.stanford.edu/2005/06/14/jobs-061505/

100. Steger MF, Kashdan TB. "Depression and Everyday Social Activity, Belonging, and Well-Being". *Journal of counseling psychology*. 2009;56(2):289-300. And also see the World Health Organization's report Mental Health and Work: Impact, issues and good practices.

101. In fact, I've taken to eliminating disposable coffee cups and their plastic lids from my life. Rather than walk out with the future trash in my hand, I ask for a ceramic mug and take a few minutes out just to sit down and enjoy the coffee. Good for the planet, and good for me too.

102. See more on this in Chapter 39: 'I'm Gonna Be...'.

103. "Constitution of WHO."

104. That dreaded super-exhaustion that shifts us towards depression. See the section 'A Word on Wellbeing' at the start of Part One.

105. Research now has compelling evidence that sitting for more than four hours a day leads to enzymes responsible for burning harmful blood fats shutting down, reduced calorie burning, disrupted blood sugar levels, increased insulin and blood pressure levels, and your leg muscles switching off. It doesn't matter what your physical ability is – as a result of all that sitting around you'll have an increased risk of heart disease, diabetes, obesity, cancer, dementia, depression, muscle degeneration and general back ache. Get off your ass and have a look at www.getbritainstanding.org.

106. Thanks to Mark Shayler for this little idea. Perhaps the most earth-shattering wake-up call I've ever had – nice one, Mark. Get yourself a copy of Mark's book *Do Disrupt: Change the Status Quo or Become It* (London: The Do Book Co, 2017) – it's brilliant.

107. Seneca, *De Brevitate Vitae (On the Shortness of Life)*. Google it and settle down for the read of your life.

RESOURCES

In addition to checking out the books, documents and websites mentioned in this book, you can also log on to **www.TheWellbeingBook.info** to access articles, downloads, posters and much more to **master your mind, boost your body and supercharge your soul**.

An exclusive *The Wellbeing Book Manifesto* poster and screensaver are available only to *The Wellbeing Book* readers – download these with the code **ButFirstCoffee**

FURTHER READING

Despite the advances of mobile technology, fast-and-light reportage and bite-sized news, I firmly believe in the power of a good book.

Here are some suggestions if you'd like to further your explorations into the topics introduced in this book.

MIND

Charles Duhigg, *The Power of Habit: Why We Do What We Do, and How to Change* (New York : Random House, 2012).

Steve Hilton, *More Human* (New York: Public Affairs, 2016).

Chuck Klosterman, *But What If We're Wrong?* (New York: Penguin, 2017).

BODY

Matthew Crawford, *The Case for Working with Your Hands: Or Why Office Work Is Bad for Us and Fixing Things Feels Good (New York: Viking, 2009).*

Gavin Francis, *Adventures in Being Human (Edinburgh: Canongate, 2015).*

Alastair Humphreys, *Micro-adventures (London: William Collins, 2014).*

SOUL

Eben Alexander, *Proof of Heaven (New York: Simon & Schuster, 2012).*

Alastair Bonnett, *Off the Map (London: Aurum Press, 2014).*

Richard Sennett, *Together: The Rituals, Pleasures and Politics of Cooperation (New Haven CT: Yale University Press, 2014).*

ACKNOWLEDGMENTS, BIG THANKS AND LOVE

While my name is on the cover of this book, the fingerprints of many cover its pages.

Rewind to 2014: the *Escape* crew for facilitating a tough decision to break free.

Dad, Jeb, Davidoff and the Sharman–Salter clan for love and turbo-charging my wellbeing. You guys really, really, are *the best*. Thanks for being *my* family.

Eagle #1 for always finding the thermals with me, Super-Hari for ideas and coolness, Emer for always telling it straight, Lorenzo for inspiration, Louis for the tunes, Nigel for supplies and the inimitable Trelawney Hart for high spirits. Powering on with Steve-Oats. And DJ Toph in the mix – *yes mate!*

Dr Edgar Schein, Professor Andrew Hopkins, Professor Erik Hollnagel, Dr Frank Furedi, Dr Leandro Herrero, Professor Geert Hofstede, Dr Evelyn Kortum and Professor Paul Slovic for inspired thinking and deep learning. Always more than you know.

The *Fleming.* team, and Ben G, and Aron, and Sven, and Louis, and Nick, and Thomas, Jens and Sam for putting me on your stages and giving me airtime with awesome audiences. And especially Kate and Michal for making it rock.

Thanks to Niki, Sara and Sally at LID for faith, fun and full support.

And last here in this list, but *never* least, all of our clients past, present and future – I'm looking after my mind, body and soul for you as well as me. Thanks for working with me and the team.

(Well, I have to draw the line somewhere!)

ABOUT THE AUTHOR

ANDREW SHARMAN is an in-demand consultant, speaker and coach who works globally with Fortune 500 companies to improve their culture and enable excellence. His clients include the fastest Formula One racing team, the most sophisticated fashion brands, the world's coolest tech companies and the tastiest chocolate-makers, as well as non-governmental organizations (NGOs) including the International Trade Centre, the United Nations and the World Health Organization – for which he's been running wellbeing and personal resilience programmes for several years.

Andrew is professor of leadership and culture and programme director at CEDEP (the European Centre for Executive Development) in Fontainebleau, France, and also teaches at Caltech (the California Institute of Technology) in the US and on post-graduate programmes at the University of Zurich, Switzerland.

He is chairman of the board of the Institute of Leadership & Management and holds non-executive roles for several NGOs and charities.

To maintain his wellbeing, Andrew likes reading, one-minute workouts and swimming with sharks.

**Get in touch for a chat about your wellbeing or
to discuss training and speaking opportunities:**

www.thewellbeingbook.info
www.andrewsharman.com
@ads_sharman
www.linkedin.com/in/adsharman

Also by the same author:
Working Well, Maverick Eagle Press, 2018
Naked Safety, Routledge, 2018
Mind Your Own Business, Maverick Eagle Press, 2017
Safety & Health for Business, IOSH Publications, 2017
Safety Savvy, Maverick Eagle Press, 2016
From Accidents to Zero, Second Edition, Routledge, 2015
From Accidents to Zero, Maverick Eagle Press, 2014

25TH
LID ANNIVERSARY

Sharing knowledge since 1993

- 1993 Madrid
- 2008 Mexico DF and Monterrey
- 2010 London
- 2011 New York and Buenos Aires
- 2012 Bogotá
- 2014 Shanghai